Located in Paducah, Kentucky, the American Quilter's Society (AQS) is dedicated to promoting the accomplishments of today's quilters. Through its publications and events, AQS strives to honor today's quiltmakers and their work and to inspire future creativity and innovation in quiltmaking.

EXECUTIVE BOOK EDITOR: ELAINE H. BRELSFORD
BOOK EDITOR: KATHY DAVIS
COPY EDITOR: CHRYSTAL ABHALTER
PROOFREADER: JOANN TREECE
ILLUSTRATIONS: SARAH BOZONE, LYNDA SMITH
GRAPHIC DESIGN: SARAH BOZONE
COVER DESIGN: MICHAEL BUCKINGHAM
QUILT PHOTOGRAPHY: CHARLES R. LYNCH

All rights reserved. No part of this book may be reproduced, stored in any retrieval system, or transmitted in any form, or by any means including but not limited to electronic, mechanical, photocopy, recording or otherwise, without the written consent of the author and publisher. Patterns may be copied for personal use only, including the right to enter contests; quilter should seek written permission from the author and pattern designer before entering. Credit must be given to the author, pattern designer, and publisher on the quilt label and contest entry form. Written permission from author, pattern designer, and publisher must be sought to raffle or auction quilts made from this book. While every effort has been made to ensure that the contents of this publication are as accurate and correct as possible, no warranty is provided nor results guaranteed. Since the author and AQS have no control over individual skills or choice of materials and tools, they do not assume responsibility for the use of this information.

Additional copies of this book may be ordered from the American Quilter's Society, PO Box 3290, Paducah, KY 42002-3290, or online at www.AmericanQuilter.com.

Text and illustrations © 2014, Author, Teri Henderson Tope
Artwork © 2014, American Quilter's Society

American Quilter's Society
PO Box 3290 • Paducah, KY 42002-3290
Fax 270-898-1173 • email: orders@AQSquilt.com

Library of Congress Cataloging-in-Publication Data Pending

# Dedication

My book is dedicated to those who celebrate life with me!

Tim Tope, my partner in crime—whose super power is to always know what time it is.

Andrea, Erin, and Hannah—your ability to put up with Crazy Mom, Grumpy Mom, and Stressed-Out Mom always amazes me.

Tucker and Hudson—being Grandma Teri is the best job I have ever had.

QuiltTrends quilt shop—you came through when I needed you the most. You inspire me, feed my creativity daily, and have given me my second home.

And my quilting community—I can't imagine a life without quilting in it.

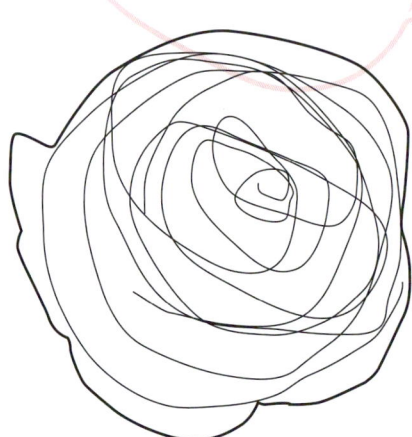

# Introduction

Growing up I can't remember an occasion that wasn't celebrated with family and food. My large, loud Italian/German/American family celebrated everything and not just holidays. We partied on snow days with snow ice cream or caramel corn popcorn balls, football Saturdays with homemade chili and corn bread, home-baked cookies on the first day of school, or Mom making dip eggs on a Saturday morning (sunny-side up with toast), and my favorite—when Dad got the hankering for something cold and creamy, we knew a tin roof sundae was not far away.

Now I became a quilter, not a gourmet cook. The fact that I don't create amazing gourmet meals doesn't mean I can't look good microwaving a frozen one and I can make a mean pot of chili. A simple bowl of soup becomes a party when eaten on a custom-made place mat with a cloth napkin. Even washing the dishes can be fun while wearing a vintage-style apron. Okay, maybe not fun but you look great! This book celebrates the kitchen and the meals and memories created there.

My goal for the apron designs in this book is to have as few open or unfinished seams as possible. I also like to line them with lightweight woven 100% cotton fusible interfacing. Lazy Girl Designs Face-It Soft and Pellon® Shape-Flex® are my favorites. These give more substance to the quilter's cottons I love to sew and create an apron that needs little or no pressing when laundered.

I hope you find the perfect way to embellish your celebration.

Bon Appetit!

Teri Henderson Tope

# Contents

**Projects**

Everyday Celebrations..................................................4
  Teri's Pot Holder and Mug Rug ........................ 5
  Table Runner ....................................................... 7
  Wine Glass Cozy ................................................. 9
  Mom's Coasters ................................................. 12
  Monsters ............................................................. 14
  Decorative Banner ........................................... 19
  Baby Bib .............................................................. 22

Garden Party Celebrations ...................................... 24
  Garden Party Apron — Adult ........................ 25
  Garden Party Apron — Child ........................ 28
  Tea Cozy ............................................................. 32
  Place Mats .......................................................... 34
  Napkins ............................................................... 36
  Round Casserole Carrier ................................. 37

Retro Mama Celebrations ........................................ 42
  Retro Mama Apron .......................................... 43
  Rectangular Casserole Carrier ....................... 48
  Oven Mitt ........................................................... 50
  Hanging Kitchen Towel .................................. 52

Tailgate Celebrations ................................................ 54
  Tailgate Apron — Adult .................................. 55
  Tailgate Apron — Child .................................. 60
  Insulated Bottle Carrier .................................. 63

Sweetheart Celebration ........................................... 68
  Sweetheart Apron ............................................ 69

**Tips and Techniques** .............................................. 74

**About the Author** ................................................... 79

# Everyday Celebrations

Let's face it! Housework, cooking, and cleaning are sometimes just not fun. Understatement! It has to be done or you will end up with your own reality TV show. My trick for dealing with the drudgery? Make it pretty! Note that I have been known to forego the cooking and cleaning part of this statement in order to make it pretty. Priorities!

Everyday Celebrations

# Teri's Pot Holder and Mug Rug

One afternoon I decided to make cookies and realized all of my lovely pot holders had disappeared. I soon found them in my teenage daughter Hannah's room and next to my husband's computer. Slightly larger than the traditional pot holder, it seems they are just the right size to carry that mug of hot chocolate or a microwaved treat to their respective resting places. So, the cookies waited for another day and back to the sewing room I went. For you see, I would rather sew than bake.

9" x 9" finished size
I suggest you construct these by assembly line and make several at a time.

## Supplies

- (1) 10" x 10" fabric for the backing
- Assorted 10" strips of fabric of varying widths from 1½" to 3" (Jelly Roll™ strips work great)
- (1) 10" x 10" Insul~Bright® from The Warm Company®
- (1) 10" x 10" cotton batting
- Sewing thread
- 1½ yards of ½" double-fold bias binding. See pages 75–77 to make home sewn binding.
- Sewing machine with a walking foot
- Rotary cutter, ruler, and mat
- Basic sewing supplies

Teri Henderson Tope • Home Sewn Celebrations

Everyday Celebrations

## Construction

This is a quilt-as-you-go project. Make a sandwich of the backing, Insul~Bright, and cotton batting. Pin baste this sandwich with a few quilter's pins. Place the quilt sandwich, backing-side down, batting-side up on the sewing table. Place 1 strip of fabric right-side up on the edge of the sandwich.

Place a second strip with right sides together on top of the first strip. With the walking foot, sew a ¼" seam through all thicknesses.

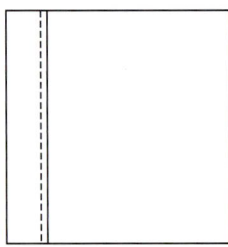

Remove from machine and place on ironing board. Press the strips open.

Place a third strip of fabric with right sides together over the second strip. Sew a ¼" seam and then press open.

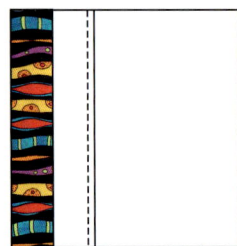

Continue to sew more strips onto the sandwich until it has been entirely covered.

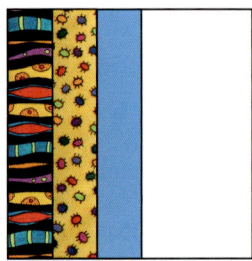

Using a rotary cutter, square and trim the block to a 9" x 9" square.

Attach the binding to the square leaving an 8" tail.

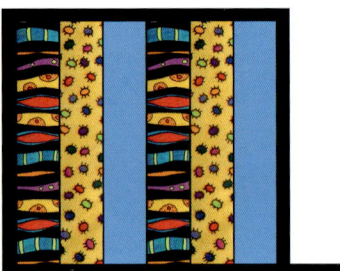

Attach the tail to the edge of the block to create a loop for hanging.

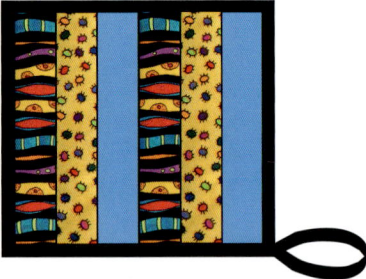

Now be prepared for pot holders to disappear. I suggest making a bunch of these.

Teri Henderson Tope — Home Sewn Celebrations

Everyday Celebrations

# Table Runner

Well then, I had a thought! Why not create a giant pot holder/table runner to rest those cookie sheets on? You know, the cookies I did not make because I was sewing. Why not put Insul~Bright in the table runner. Eureka! No more scrambling during a buffet-style meal to place all those hot dishes on coasters or trivits. When serving a family meal I can now place the hot dishes down the center of the table and passing the potatoes just got a whole lot easier. A couple of hours later I finished my first of many coaster mats or insulated table runners. I now make all my table runners with a layer of batting and Insul~Bright.

15" x 36" finished size
This is the same concept as the pot holder and mug rug, just bigger.

## Supplies

- (1) 18" x 40" rectangle of fabric for backing
- Assorted strips of fabric of varying widths from 1½" to 3" (Jelly Rolls work great!)
- (1) 18" x 40" rectangle of Insul~Bright
- (1) 18" x 40" rectangle of cotton batting
- Sewing machine with a walking foot
- Sewing thread
- 3⅓ yards of 2½" double-fold bias binding. See pages 75–77 to make home sewn binding.
- Rotary cutter, ruler, and mat
- Basic sewing supplies

Everyday Celebrations

## Construction

This is a quilt-as-you-go project. Sandwich the backing, Insul~Bright, and cotton batting. Pin baste the sandwich with a few quilter's pins. Place one strip of fabric right-side up on the edge of the sandwich.

Place a strip with right sides together on top of the first strip. Using the walking foot sew a ¼" seam through all thicknesses and along the edges of the strips.

Remove the tablerunner from the sewing machine and place on an ironing board. Press the strips open.

Place a third strip of fabric with right sides together over the second strip. Sew a ¼" seam and then press the strips open. Continue this step until the entire sandwich has been covered.

Periodically lay a ruler across the project to check the placement of the strips and keep them straight. Slight adjustments can be made throughout the project to keep everything in line.

Using a rotary cutter, square and trim the table runner to 14" x 36".

Attach the binding to the table runner.

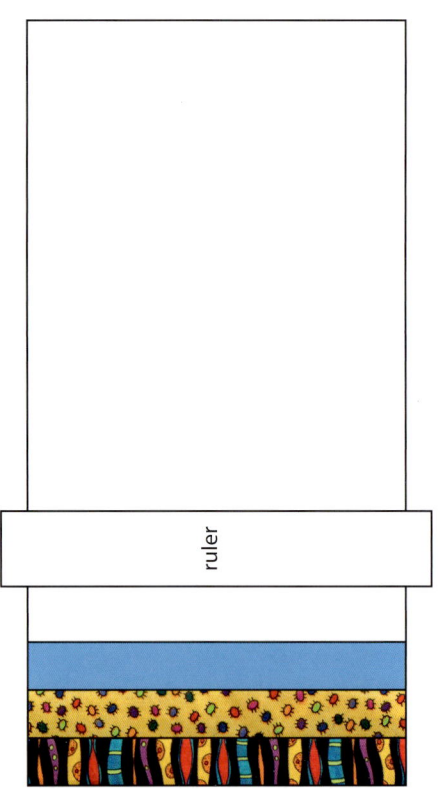

### TIP

This project can be customized for any length or width you might need. Just be sure to add extra length and width to the sandwich measurement so you can square it up after the strips are sewn together.

Teri Henderson Tope — Home Sewn Celebrations

Everyday Celebrations

# Wine Glass Cozy

Several years ago my mother gave me a set of homemade coasters. They worked great for sweaty glasses of ice tea or a mug of coffee, but not so well for a wine glass. At a formal function with my husband, I noticed cute little paper circles attached to the wine glasses with the company logo imprinted on them. A lightbulb went off and I couldn't wait to get home to the sewing room. By the next morning a lovely row of wine glasses graced my kitchen counter, each with its own cute little cozy. These wine glass cozies are sure to be a hit with your friends and family—an easy addition to a good bottle of wine for a lovely gift. Vary the fabrics and they become wine glass IDs.

## Supplies

Makes one wine glass cozy—of course, you really can't make just one. This is a great stash buster!

- (5) 5" fabric circles. Mix and match your favorite colors.
- 12" of ½" rickrack
- Pinking shears
- Sewing thread
- Fabric marking tool
- Sewing machine with a walking foot
- Basic sewing supplies

Teri Henderson Tope • Home Sewn Celebrations

Everyday Celebrations

### Full Size Pattern Needed From CD

1—Wine Glass Cozy

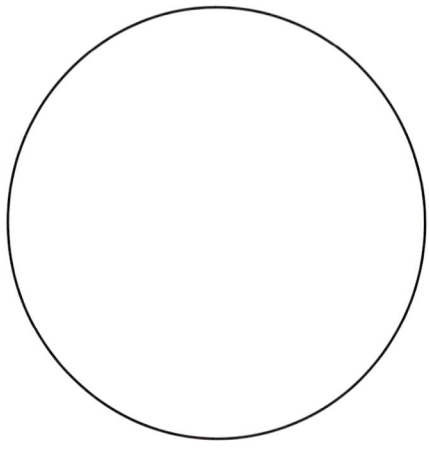

1—Wine Glass Cozy

Choose 1 circle for the bottom of the cozy. On the right side of it, sew the rickrack to the inside of this circle with a ¼" seam. See Tips and Techniques on page 74 for information on attaching rickrack.

Take the remaining 4 circles to the ironing board. Fold each in half with wrong sides together and press.

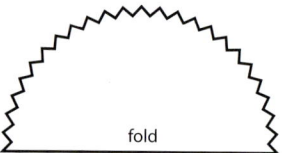

Place the cozy bottom right-side up on your work surface. Place a folded circle over the bottom so it overlaps half of the bottom of the cozy with the fold toward the center of the circle. Pin the folded circle in place.

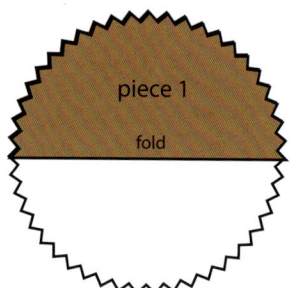

### Construction

Trace the wine glass cozy pattern onto the back of the fabrics and cut out 5 circles with pinking shears. This will save you the step of clipping the curves around the sewn circle. You will thank me when you turn these babies right-side out.

Place a second folded circle on top of the first folded circle, overlapping half of it with the fold toward the center. Pin the second circle into place.

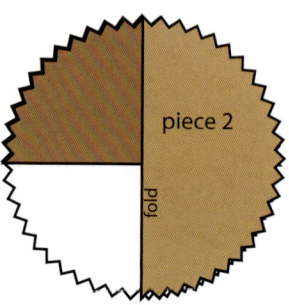

Teri Henderson Tope • Home Sewn Celebrations

Everyday Celebrations

Place a third folded circle on top of the second folded circle, overlapping half of it with the fold toward the center. Pin the third circle into place.

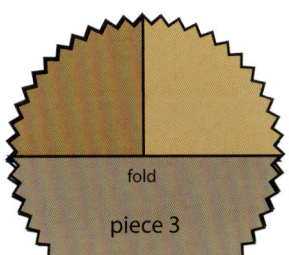

Place the fourth folded circle on top of the third circle, overlapping half of it. Tuck one half of the fourth circle under the first circle. The fold will be toward the center. Pin the fourth circle into place.

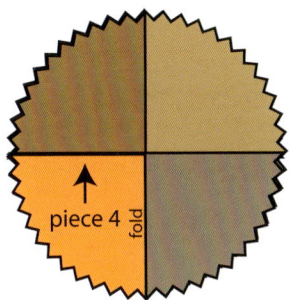

Flip the cozy over and with the walking foot, sew through all the thicknesses using the seam line previously sewn for the rickrack.

Turn the cozy inside out and gently pull on the rickrack to create a perfect circle. Press.

Insert a wine glass through the folds of the cozy and pour a glass of your favorite wine. Enjoy!

Teri Henderson Tope · Home Sewn Celebrations

Everyday Celebrations

# Mom's Coasters

If you are interested in knowing how to make my mom's quick coasters, she has nicely allowed me to include this pattern. Thanks Mom, love you more!

## Supplies

Makes one coaster—these are kind of like potato chips. How can you make just one?

- (6) 6" x 6" squares of fabric. Mix and match your favorite colors.
- (1) 6" x 6" square of cotton quilt batting
- Sewing thread
- Sewing machine with a walking foot
- Rotary cutter, ruler, and mat
- Basic sewing supplies

## Full Size Pattern Needed From CD

2—Mom's Coasters

2—Mom's Coaster

## Construction

Choose two fabric squares for the coaster bottom. One square will be on the inside and other will be on the outside of the coaster.

Take the remaining 4 squares to the ironing board. Fold each square in half with right sides together.

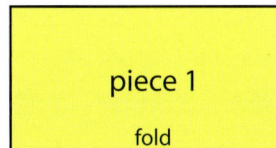

On a work surface, layer a bottom square right-side down (this will become the interior square), the quilt batting square, and the remaining bottom square right-side up.

Place a folded square over the bottom square, overlapping half of it with raw edges together. The fold will be on the interior edge. Pin into place.

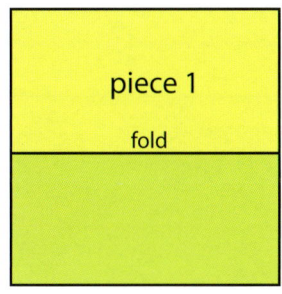

Place a second folded square over the first folded square, overlapping half of it with raw edges together. The fold will be toward the interior edge. Pin into place.

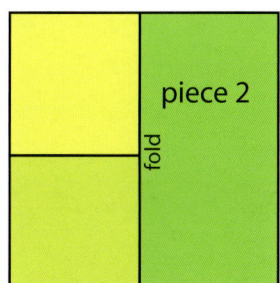

Place a third folded square over the second square, overlapping half of it with raw edges together. The fold will be toward the interior edge. Pin into place.

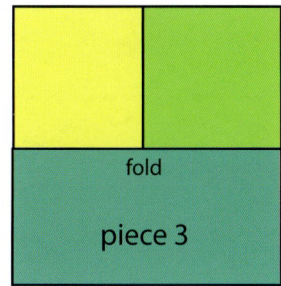

Place the last folded square over the third square, overlapping half of it. Tuck one half of the fourth square under the first folded square. The fold will be toward the interior edge. Pin into place.

With a walking foot sew through all the thicknesses around the edges of the square using a generous ¼" seam allowance.

Clip the corners to reduce bulk.

Turn the coaster inside out and press. The corners of the coaster will be slightly rounded because of all the thickness of the fabric and batting.

A set of four tied together with a ribbon makes a wonderful gift, don't you think?

Teri Henderson Tope — Home Sewn Celebrations

Everyday Celebrations

# Monsters

You may wonder why I have included monsters in this book. Our first grandchild is a boy—Tucker Samuel Linhart. For his second birthday my daughter chose a monster theme. Perfect for any two-year-old, don't you think? Grandma Teri decided she should make treat sacks for this little sweetheart. But not just any treat sack, this is my grandson, for goodness sake!

A few hours in the sewing room and the first little monster made it into the world. A quick chat with my daughter and, gulp, 16 more monsters were on their way. Each had a scrappy little pocket to hold monster treats (gummy fruit snacks) and was ready to be adopted by Tucker's little friends. While I was madly stitching monsters, my 16-year-old, Miss Hannah, wandered into the sewing room stating, "These are cute. Can I have one?" I was soon machine-assembly-line stitching a couple of dozen cute little monsters and using up lots of fun scraps in the process.

At Tucker's party my daughter placed the monsters into a basket and added a cute little sign, "Free to a Good Home."

Everyday Celebrations

## Supplies

Makes one monster—although from experience, you can never make just one.

**Small Monster**
- (2) 9" x 11" rectangles of Minky, flannel, or fleece for the body
- (1) 8" x 5" rectangle of fabric for the pocket
- (1) 4" x 6½" rectangle of fabric for the face

**Large Monster**
- (2) 7" x 14" rectangles of Minky, flannel, or fleece for the body
- (1) 4" x 10" rectangle of fabric for the pocket
- (1) 5" x 5" square of fabric for the face

**Additional Supplies Needed to Make Either Monster**
- (8) 4" x 3" assorted scraps for the arms and legs
- (1) 8" x 10" rectangle of lightweight fusible web
- ⅓ of a bag of fiberfill stuffing
- Sewing machine with a walking foot
- ½ yard of ¼" ribbon for the hair
- Needle and thread to attach the button eyes
- Pinking shears
- Scraps of fabrics for the eyes and cheeks
- (2) buttons—if making monsters for very small children, use scraps of black fabric
- Thread to match
- Pencil
- Monster treats to hide in the pockets
- Basic sewing supplies

## Full Size Patterns Needed From CD

3—Small Monster Body
4—Small Monster Face
5—Small Monster Pocket
9—Monster Arm and Leg

6—Large Monster Body
7—Large Monster Face
8—Large Monster Pocket
9—Monster Arm and Leg

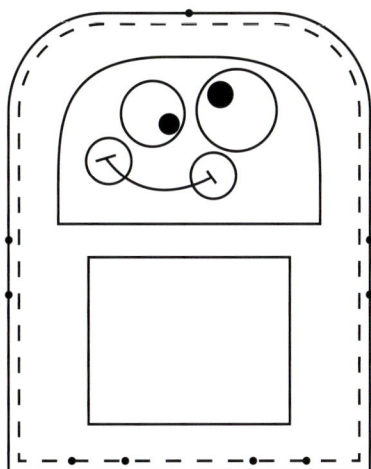

3—Small Monster Body

Teri Henderson Tope · Home Sewn Celebrations

Everyday Celebrations

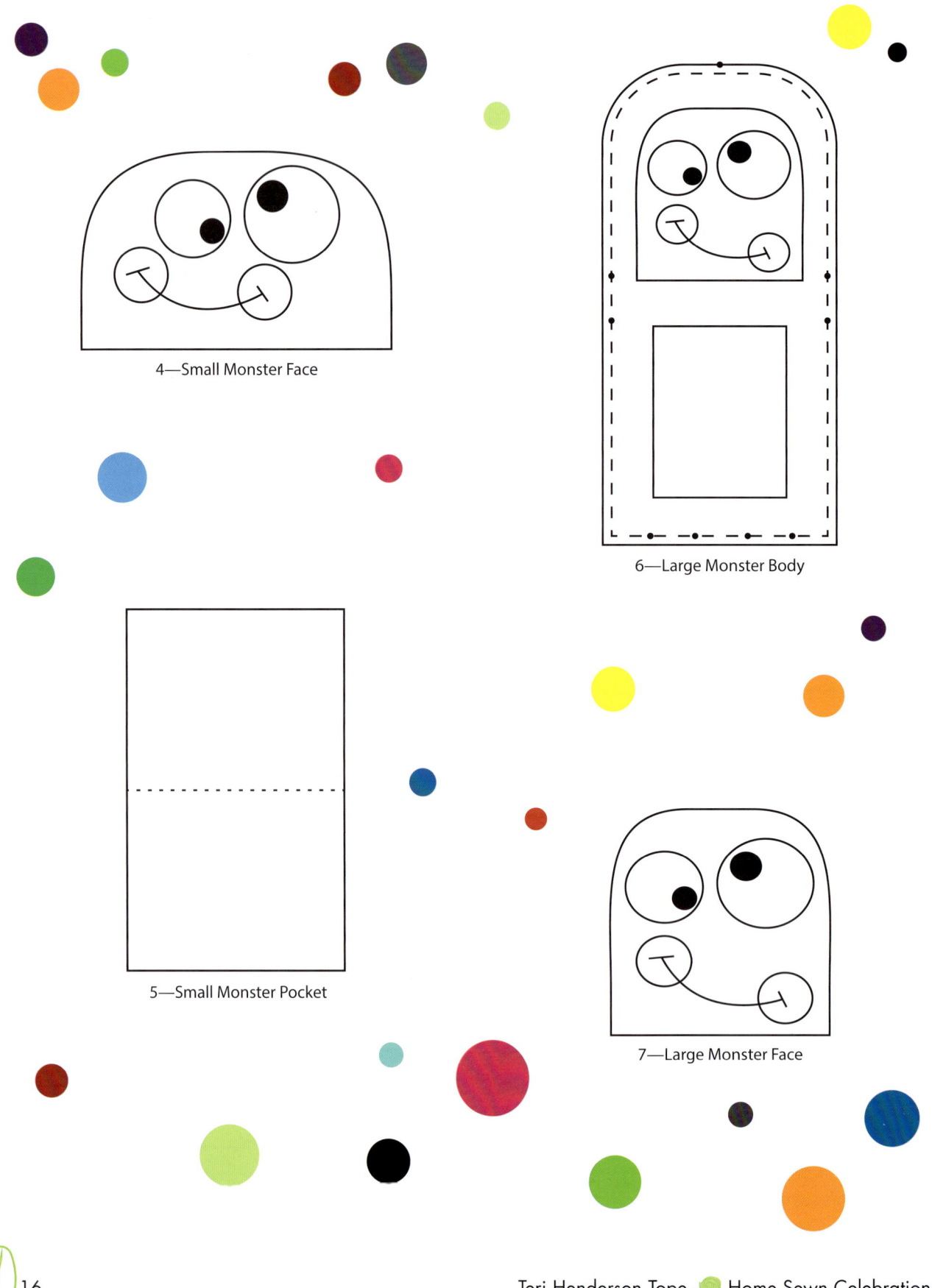

Everyday Celebrations

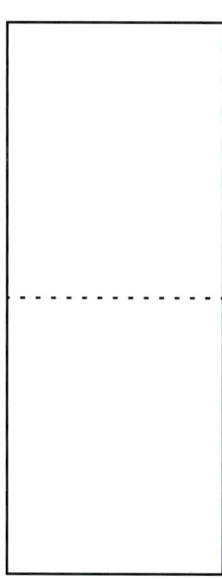

8—Large Monster Pocket

### TIP

If you have a Clover® Mini Iron, please use it to attach the fusible pieces. A large hot iron will press out Minky's textured pattern.

## Construction

Both monsters are made using the same assembly steps.

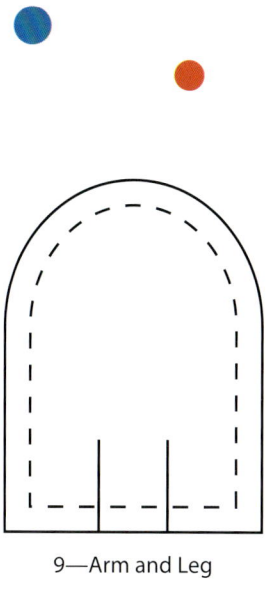

9—Arm and Leg

Teri Henderson Tope    Home Sewn Celebrations

17

Everyday Celebrations

### Eyes, Cheeks, and Face

Trace the eyes, cheeks, and face onto the paper side of the fusible web and roughly cut out.

Fuse the eyes, cheeks, and face fusible web pieces to the back of appropriately colored fabrics.

Cut each piece out on the pattern line. I used pinking shears to cut out the face piece.

Remove the paper from the eyes and cheeks. Do not remove the paper backing from the face just yet.

Place the face pattern on the ironing board right-side up. Arrange the eyes and cheeks on the face and fuse per the manufacturer's directions.

Raw-edge appliqué to finish the edges of the eyes and cheeks.

Add the smiley mouth by using a satin stitch on the sewing machine.

Remove the paper from the back of the now-completed face and place it on the monster's front body. Press to fuse the face to the body. Finish the face using a straight stitch just inside the pinked edge.

Hand sew the buttons to finish the eyes.

### Pocket

Fold the pocket fabric in half with wrong sides together. Press. The folded edge will be the top of the pocket.

Place the pocket on the monster body front as shown on the pattern.

Topstitch along the sides of the pocket to secure it to the monster body. Make sure to backstitch at the top of the pocket.

### Arms and Legs

Pin the arms and legs pattern to 4" x 3" scraps of fabric and cut out. You will need 8 of these pieces—2 for each arm or leg.

Place 2 fabric pieces right sides together and stitch a ¼" seam. Make 4 sets.

Clip the curved edge. I use my handy pinking shears.

Turn right-side out and press.

Make a small pleat on the open end of each arm and leg. Pin them to the body as indicated on the pattern.

### Hair

Loop the ribbon around three fingers.

Place this loop at the top of the monster's head on the right side of the fabric with raw edges together and baste it in the seam line to hold it in place. The ribbon hair will hang in the center of the face until the body is sewn together.

### Assemble the Monster

Do you feel a little like Dr. Frankenstein right now?

Carefully pin the front and the back of the monster right sides together. Make sure the arms, legs, and hair are straight and in their proper places.

Using the walking foot, stitch a ¼" seam around the sides and top of the monster. Leave the bottom of the monster open for the stuffing.

Turn monster right-side out and stuff.

Fold a ¼" seam allowance inward at the bottom and pin to hold the opening closed. Whipstitch the seam by hand or stitch a ⅛" seam on the outside of the body by machine.

Place a treat in the monster's pocket and make a kid of any size smile.

Everyday Celebrations

# Decorative Banner

What started out as a little project for Grandson Tucker's first birthday has grown to encompass all of our holidays and celebrations. When asked by daughter Andrea to create a bunting for Tucker's birthday, how could I say no? A couple of hours in the sewing room and—Tada! Bunting! And when little Hudson came along, Grandma Teri made one announcing his name for the nursery wall.

## Supplies

Makes one letter

- (1) 9" x 10" rectangle of fabric for the front of the banner flag
- (1) 9" x 10" rectangle of fabric for the backing of the banner flag
- (2) 9" x 10" rectangles of fusible web—one for the flag and one for the fused letter
- (1) 9" x 10" rectangle of fabric for the letter
- ½" double-fold bias binding—10" for each letter used in the banner plus 30" for the ties. See pages 75–77 to make yours home sewn.
- Rotary cutter, ruler, and mat
- Pencil
- Thread to match bias tape
- Basic sewing supplies

Teri Henderson Tope    Home Sewn Celebrations

Everyday Celebrations

**Full Size Patterns Needed From CD**

10—Banner
11—Alphabet

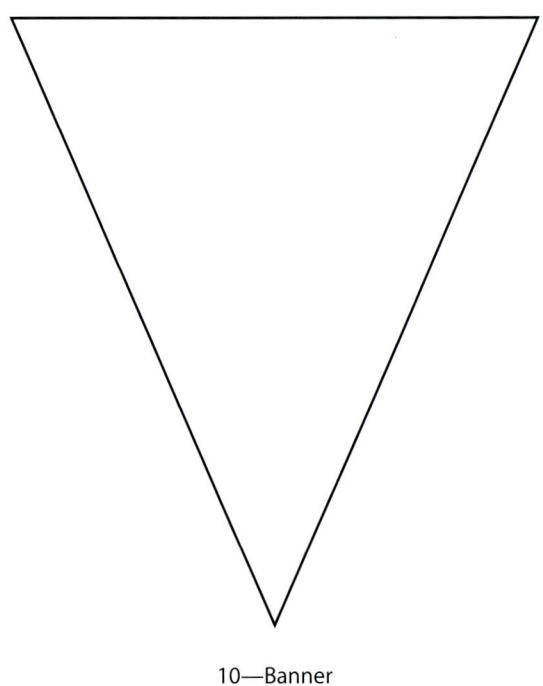

10—Banner

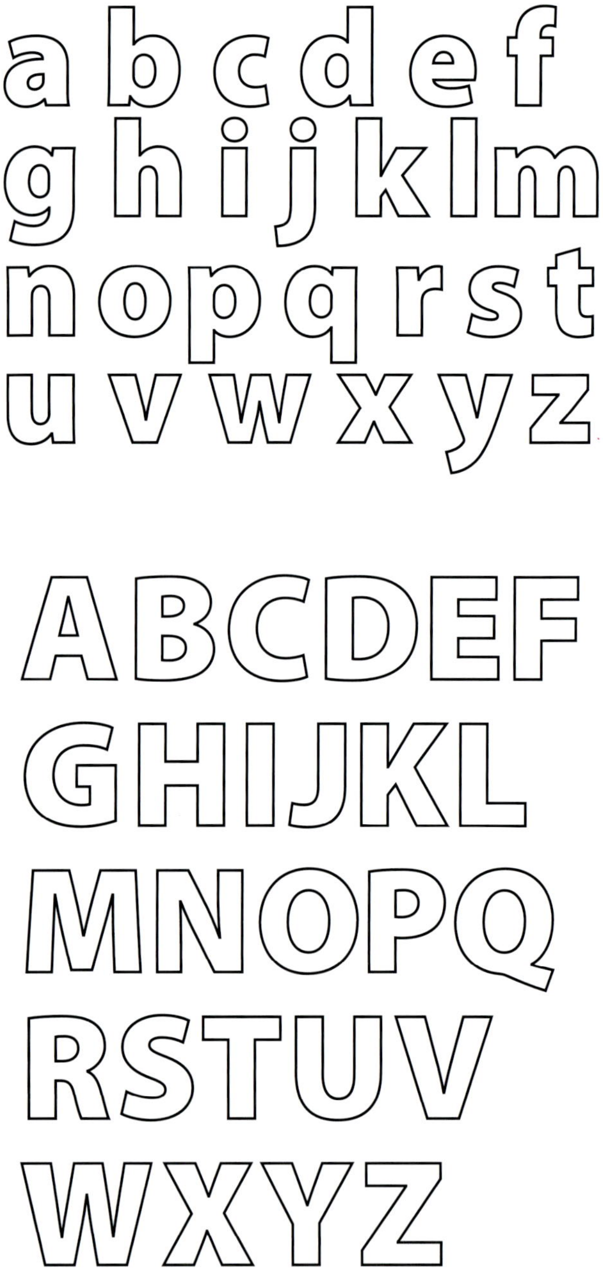

abcdef
ghijklm
nopqrst
uvwxyz

ABCDEF
GHIJKL
MNOPQ
RSTUV
WXYZ

11—Alphabet

Teri Henderson Tope — Home Sewn Celebrations

## Banner Construction

Trace the letter appliqué in reverse onto the paper side of the fusible web.

Roughly cut out the appliqué just outside the drawn line.

Fuse this shape to the wrong side of the appliqué fabric and cut out on the drawn line.

To construct the banner, fuse a 9" x 10" piece of fusible web to the banner fabric.

Remove the paper backing from the web and layer the banner back and the banner front wrong sides together. Press with an iron until the layers are securely adhered. You now have a double-sided piece of fabric.

Trace the banner pattern onto the double-sided fabric and cut the flag out with a rotary cutter.

**Banner Construction**

Lay the banners on a flat surface. The last thing we want to do is make a mistake in spelling. Been there, done that.

Measure 15" from the end of the bias tape.

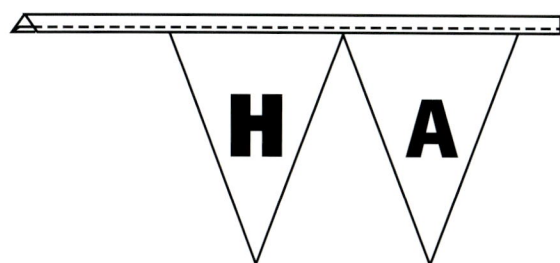

Diagram for assembling flags on a banner

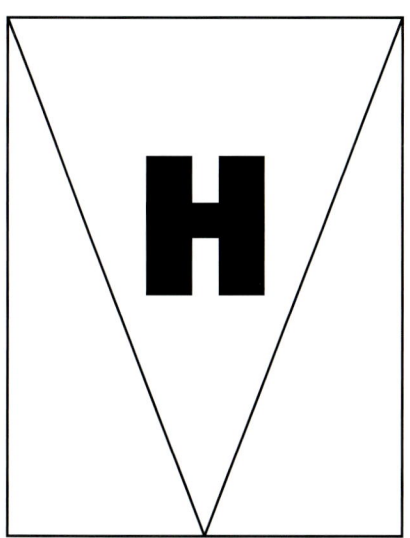

Placement of the letter and banner flag pattern

Place the first banner into the open edge of the bias tape 15" from the end and secure it with pins.

Sew along the bias tape using a ⅛" seam to create a tie. Then continue sewing along the tape to attach the first banner to the bias tape.

Do not remove it from the sewing machine. If your sewing machine has the "needle down" option, now is the time to use it.

Stop at the edge of the first banner and carefully place the next banner into the open edge of the bias tape.

Continue sewing along this edge, placing each banner into the bias fold as you go, until all of the banners are encased in the bias tape.

Continue sewing an additional 15" along the bias tape after the last banner to finish the tie.

Fuse the fabric letter to the banner front.

Sew the edge of the appliquéd letter with a decorative stitch, if needed.

Repeat the above steps for each letter in the banner.

Everyday Celebrations

### TIP
Make a double-sided banner, such as JOY on one side and BOO on the other. Other banner suggestions:
- Congrats
- She Said Yes! (for a bridal shower)
- Love • He Has Risen
- Noel • Welcome
- Girls Only • Boys Only
- Quilters Only
- Childs Name (to match that special quilt)
- Entry, Exit, Bathrooms, Classroom (reuse year after year for your quilt show)

# Baby Bib

Because I am a grandma, I decided to add this little gem to my book. Nothing makes me smile more than watching my grandbabies. And nothing could be messier than a one-year-old in a highchair, so get out all your fun fabrics and stitch up a few of these for the little ones in your life.

## Supplies

- 1 fat quarter
- ½ yard Lazy Girl Designs Face-It Soft or Pellon Shape-Flex lightweight woven 100% cotton fusible interfacing
- 2 yards ½" rickrack
- Thread to match
- Scraps for your choice of an appliqué
- 8" x 10" rectangle of lightweight fusible web
- ½" x 2" piece of Velcro® Hook and Loop Fastening Tape
- Basic sewing supplies

Teri Henderson Tope • Home Sewn Celebrations

Everyday Celebrations

## Full Size Pattern Needed From CD

12—Baby Bib

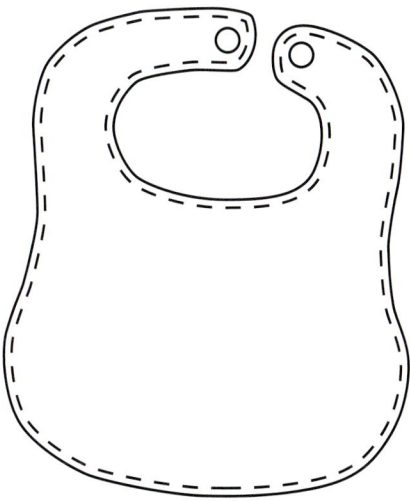

12—Baby bib pattern

Bib back

## Construction

Fuse the interfacing to the fat quarter. Pin the bib pattern to the fat quarter and cut it out.

Sew rickrack around the edge of the bib. See Tips and Techniques on page 74 for information on attaching rickrack.

Attach the Velcro to the bib using the placement marks on the pattern.

Trace an appliqué motif of your choice onto the paper side of the fusible web. If you are using letters, trace them in reverse. An alphabet, Pattern 9, is full size on the CD and is diagramed on page 20.

Roughly cut out the appliqué outside of the drawn line.

Apply the fusible web to the wrong side of the appliqué fabrics.

Cut the appliqués out on the drawn line. Remove the paper backing.

Place and fuse the appliqués to the bib front.

Stitch the raw edge of the appliqué with a satin or decorative stitch.

Tuck around the chin of your favorite child.

Teri Henderson Tope — Home Sewn Celebrations

# Garden Party Celebrations

For my 50th birthday, my quilting friends Leslie Floyd, Joanne Purcell, Liz Canty, and Dorothy Adams showed up at my house for an impromptu birthday party. Joann made an amazing lemon chiffon cake and we drank pot after pot of hot tea from my antique teacups, giggling and laughing like teenagers. A day that I really wasn't looking forward to turned into a wonderful afternoon. This collection celebrates that day.

# Garden Party Apron—Adult

Girly and flattering, this apron is sure to have all your friends green with envy. So how about stitching up a few for fun gifts? Mixing and matching the fabrics creates loads of design possibilities.

## Supplies

- 2½ yards—if constructing the apron from 1 fabric
- Yardage for mixing and matching fabrics (adjust for directional prints):
    - ⅝ yard for skirt
    - ⅓ yard for pockets
    - ½ yard for waistband and waistband ties
    - ¼ yard for bib insert
    - ⅔ yard for left and right side bibs with tie
- 1½ yard Lazy Girl Designs Face-It Soft or Pellon Shape-Flex lightweight woven 100% cotton fusible interfacing for skirt and pockets
- 5 yards rickrack for the skirt, pockets, and bib insert
- Thread to match fabrics
- Basic sewing supplies

## Full Size Patterns Needed From CD

13—Adult Apron Side Bib with Tie – Left
14—Adult Apron Side Bib with Tie – Right
15—Adult Apron Bib Insert
16—Adult Apron Skirt
17—Adult Apron Waistband
18—Adult Apron Waistband Tie
19—Adult Apron Pocket

Teri Henderson Tope • Home Sewn Celebrations

Garden Party Celebrations

13—Adult Apron Side Bib with Tie - Left

14—Adult Apron Side Bib with Tie - Right

17—Adult Apron Waistband

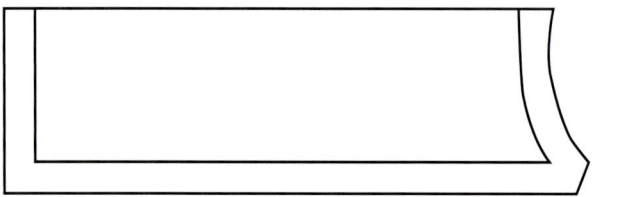
15—Adult Apron Bib Insert

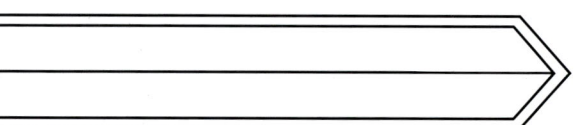
18—Adult Apron Waistband Tie

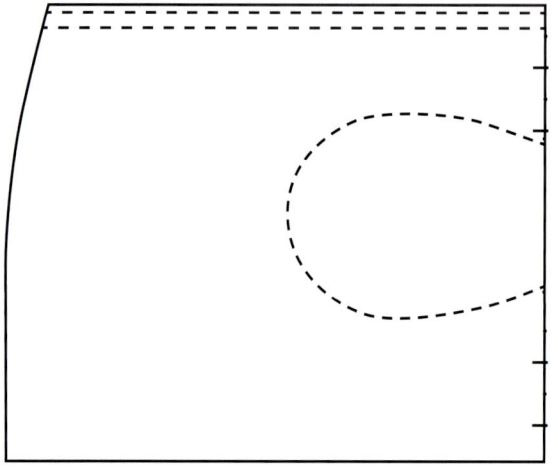
16—Adult Apron Skirt

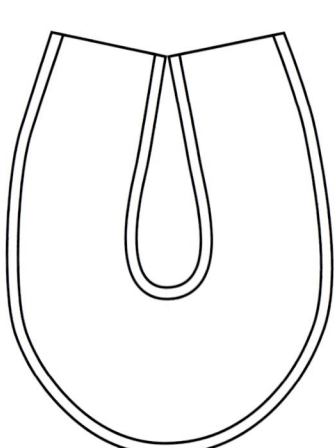
19—Adult Apron Pocket

Teri Henderson Tope — Home Sewn Celebrations

Garden Party Celebrations

## Construction

Cut pieces of interfacing larger than the skirt and pocket pattern pieces. Fuse them to the appropriate fabrics.

Using the skirt and pocket patterns, pin and cut them from the interfaced fabrics. Pin and cut the remaining pattern pieces.

Sew rickrack to the inside and outside edges of the pockets and to the sides and bottom of the skirt. See Tips and Techniques on page 74 for information on attaching rickrack.

Position and topstitch the pockets to the front of the skirt using the pocket placement marks on the skirt pattern.

To finish the left and right sides of the skirt, press a ¼" fold along the edges, then make a ½" fold and press. Sew along the fold to finish the edges.

Staystitch ¼" along the top edge of the skirt. This will stabilize the upper edge of the skirt and secure the top edge of the pockets.

Pin and staystitch the pleats at the waistband of the skirt as indicated on the pattern.

Sew rickrack to the right and left sides of the bib insert.

Pin, and with a ½" seam, sew a side bib with the ties - right to the right side of the bib insert. Pin, and with a ½" seam, sew a side bib with the ties - left to the left side of the bib insert. Press. Repeat this step to make the bib lining.

Sew the lining to the bib right sides together with a ½" seam. Clip the curves. Pinking shears work great! Turn the bib right-side out and press.

Topstitch the outside edge of the bib.

Pin and staystitch ⅛" along the bottom edge of the bib.

Press a ½" fold on the unnotched side of a waistband. This piece will become the waistband lining.

Place the bib right sides together on the other waistband matching centers of the bib and the waistband.

Place the waistband lining right side together with the wrong side of the bib matching the centers.

Sew the waistband, bib, and waistband lining together with a ½" seam the full length of the waistband.

Press the bib upward and the waistbands downward.

Pin the front waistband right sides together with the upper edge of the skirt and sew with a ½" seam allowance. Press the seam allowance toward the bib.

Fold the waistband ties right sides together and stitch with a ½" seam allowance leaving the straight end unsewn. Turn them inside out and press.

Referring to the waistband tie pattern, make a 1" pleat at the end of each tie and baste.

Match the raw edges of the waistband ties with the right side ends of the front waistband and pin.

Place the front waistband and waistband lining right sides together and stitch with a ½" seam. Turn inside out.

Stitch the bottom edge of the waistband lining to the back of the skirt.

Put on your new apron and let's party!

Teri Henderson Tope • Home Sewn Celebrations

Garden Party Celebrations

# Garden Party Apron—Child

Have a little one? Here's an apron you can coordinate with the adult's apron in the previous project. Talk about girly! Make one for your best pint-sized cooking assistant and don't forget to mix and match the fabrics.

## Supplies

- 2 yards if constructing the apron from 1 fabric
- Yardage for mixing and matching fabrics (adjust for directional prints):
    - ½ yard for skirt
    - ⅓ yard for pockets
    - ½ yard for waistband and waistband ties
    - ¼ yard for bib insert
    - ⅔ yard for left and right side bibs with tie and bib lining
- 1 yard Lazy Girl Designs Face-It Soft or Pellon Shape-Flex lightweight woven 100% cotton fusible interfacing for skirt and pockets
- 4½ yards rickrack
- Thread to match fabrics
- Basic sewing supplies

## Full Size Pattern Needed From the CD

20—Child Apron Side Bib with Tie
21—Child Apron Bib Insert
22—Child Apron Bib Lining
23—Child Apron Skirt
24—Child Apron Waistband
25—Child Apron Waistband Tie
26—Child Apron Pocket

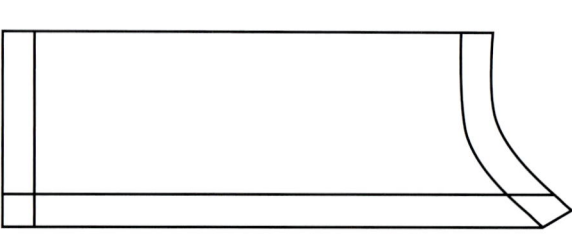

21—Child Apron Bib Insert

20—Child Apron Side Bib with Tie

Teri Henderson Tope — Home Sewn Celebrations

Garden Party Celebrations

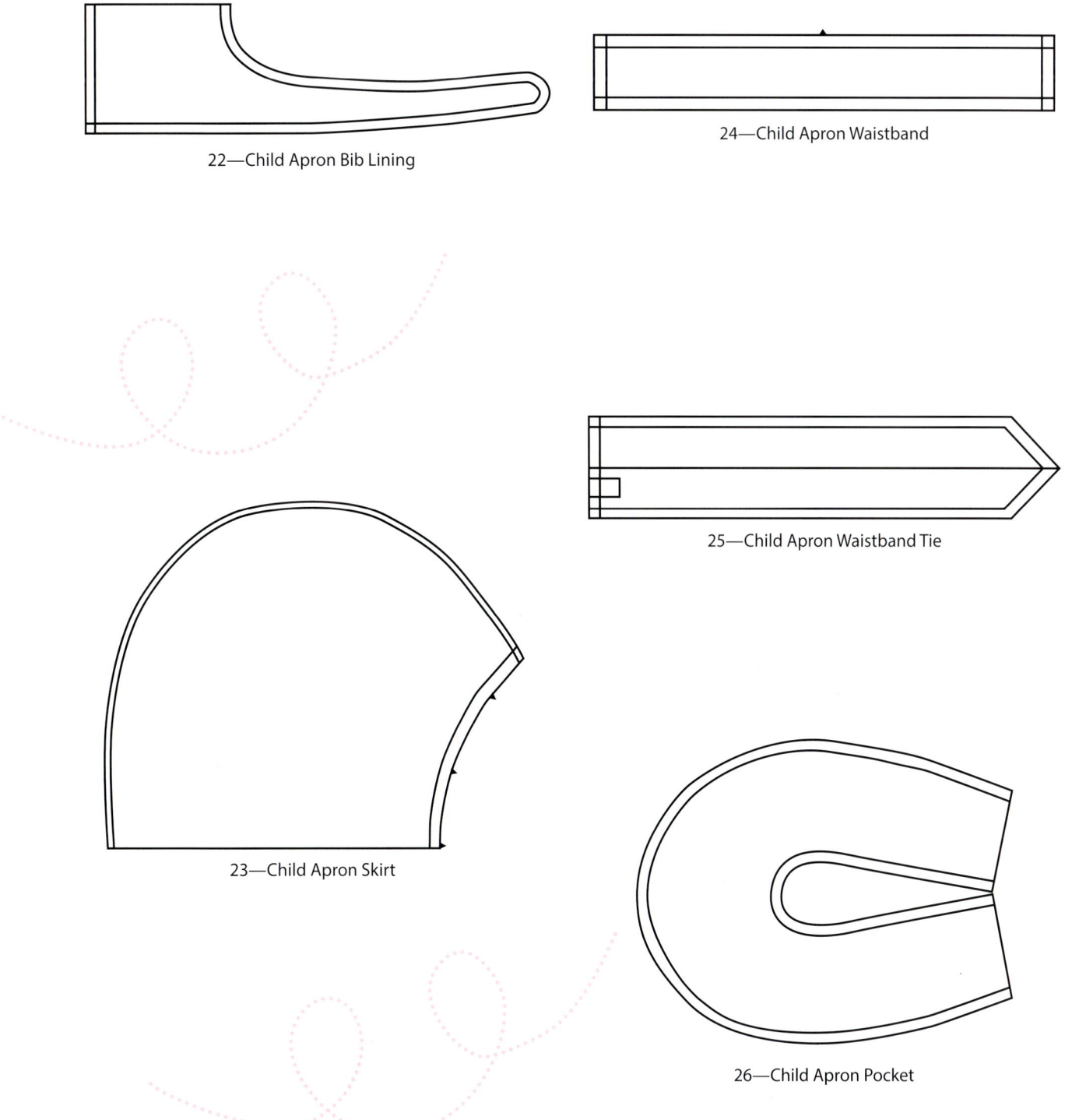

22—Child Apron Bib Lining

24—Child Apron Waistband

25—Child Apron Waistband Tie

23—Child Apron Skirt

26—Child Apron Pocket

Teri Henderson Tope  Home Sewn Celebrations

## Construction

Cut pieces of interfacing larger than the skirt and pocket pattern pieces. Fuse them to the appropriate fabrics.

Using the skirt and pocket patterns, pin and cut them from the interfaced fabrics. Pin and cut the remaining pattern pieces.

Sew rickrack to the inside and outside edges of the pockets and on the sides and bottom of the skirt. See Tips and Techniques on page 74 for information on attaching rickrack.

Pin and staystitch ⅛" along the bottom edge of the bib.

Press a ½" fold on the unnotched edge of a waistband. This piece will be the waistband lining.

Place the bib right sides together on the other waistband and match the center notches.

Place the waistband lining right side to the wrong side of the bib matching the center notches.

Sew the waistband, bib, and waistband lining together with a ½" seam the full length of the waistband.

Press the bib upward and the waistbands downward.

Pin the front waistband right sides together with the upper edge of the skirt and sew with a ½" seam allowance. Press the seam allowance toward the bib.

Fold the waistband ties right sides together and stitch with a ½" seam allowance leaving the straight end unsewn. Turn them inside out and press.

Referring to the waistband tie pattern, make a small pleat at the end of each tie and baste.

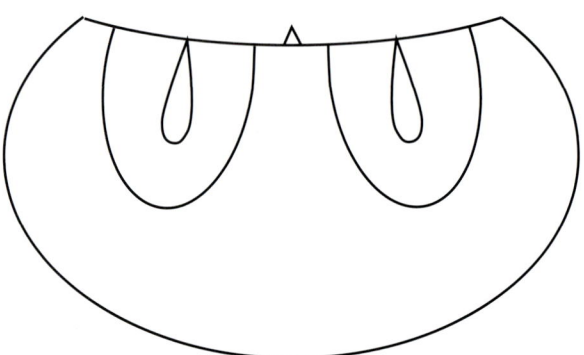

Position the pockets.

Position and topstitch the pockets to the front of the skirt using the pocket placement marks on the skirt pattern.

Staystitch ¼" along the top edge of the skirt. This will stabilize the upper curve of the skirt and secure the top edge of the pockets.

Sew rickrack to the right and left sides of the bib and the bottom of the skirt.

Pin and sew the side bib with ties to the right and left sides of the bib insert with a ½" seam. Press.

Sew the lining to the bib with right sides together with a ½" seam. Clip the curves. Pinking shears work great! Turn the bib right-side out and press.

Topstitch the outside edge of the bib.

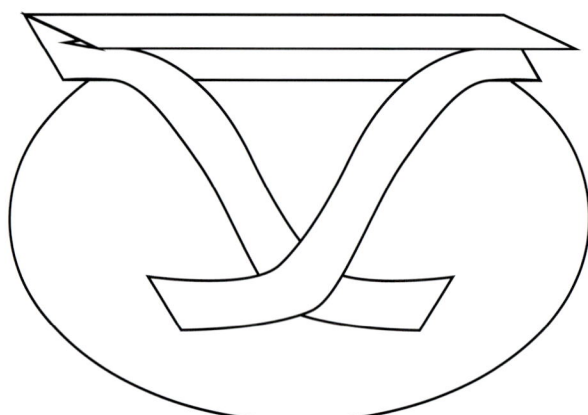

Pin the apron ties to the waistband.
Bib is not shown in order to demonstrate the position of the apron ties.

Garden Party Celebrations

Match the raw edges of the ties with the right side ends of the front waistband and pin.

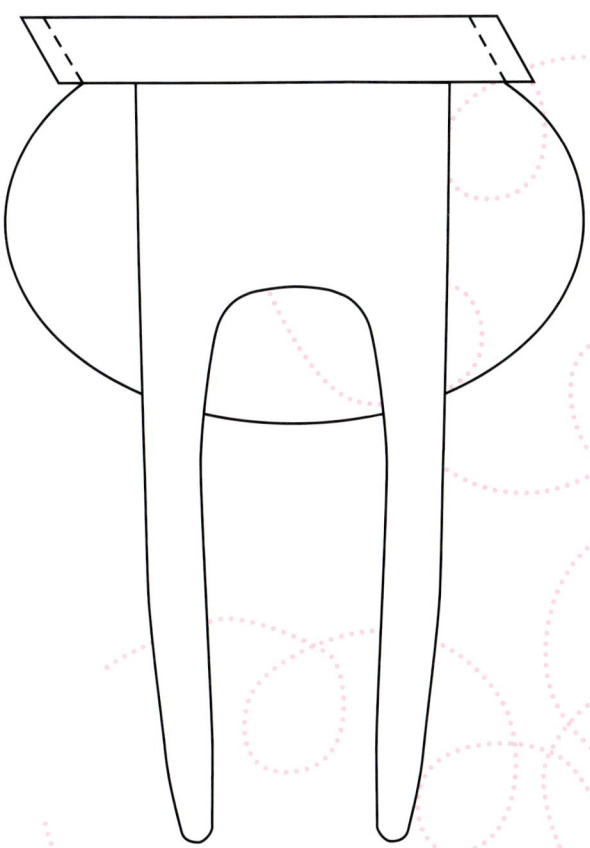

Stitch the ends of the waistband with right sides together.

Place the front waistband and waistband lining right sides together and stitch the ends with a ½" seam. Turn inside out.

Stitch the bottom edge of the waistband lining to the back of the skirt.

Dress your young cook. Isn't she beautiful?!

Garden Party Celebrations

# Tea Cozy

A well-made cup of hot tea can warm the heart and soul of any tea lover. Cover your teapot with this clever cozy to retain its warmth while also dressing up your table. This pattern was designed by my amazing friend Liz Canty.

## Supplies

- Assorted 13" strips of fabric of varying widths (1½"–3") for the outside of the tea cozy. Jelly Roll strips work great!
- 1⅓ yards double-fold bias binding. See pages 75–77 to make yours home sewn.
- ½ yard Insul~Bright cut into (2) 13" x 17" rectangles
- ½ yard fabric cut into (2) 13" x 17" rectangles for the lining
- (2) 13" x 17" rectangles of batting
- Thread to match
- Rotary cutter, ruler, and mat
- Sewing machine with walking foot
- Basic sewing supplies

Garden Party Celebrations

## Full Size Pattern Needed From CD

27—Tea Cozy

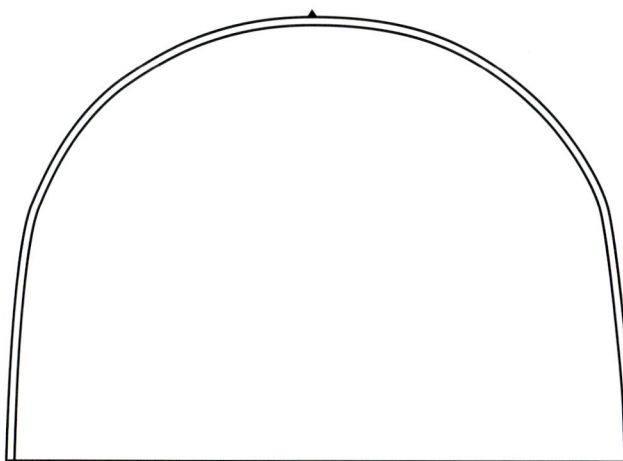

27— Tea Cozy pattern

## Construction

Sew strips of fabric together lengthwise to create (2) 13" x 17" rectangles for the front and back of the tea cozy.

On a flat surface place a lining rectangle face down. On top of it, place a rectangle of batting and then a rectangle of Insul~Bright. On top of the Insul~Bright, place a quilted rectangle face up. Repeat to make a second sandwich.

Baste and quilt the sandwiches as desired. My tea cozy was quilted in the ditch along each strip of fabric with a walking foot.

Using the Tea Cozy pattern, cut 1 piece from each of the quilted rectangles.

Cut a 6" piece of double-fold bias binding. Stitch ⅛" along the open edge to close it.

Fold the binding in half and pin it to the top of one of the tea cozy pieces at the notch, matching the raw edges. This will become the handle.

Pin the 2 quilted tea cozy pieces right sides together. The handle should be inside the 2 pieces at the top curve of the cozy.

Stitch a ¼" seam allowance with a walking foot around the curve of the top.

Sew binding to the bottom of the tea cozy.

Make a pot of tea. Cover teapot with your new tea cozy. Enjoy!

I wish that we could get together and have a cup of tea. But since we can't, when you see this, I hope you think of me.

Garden Party Celebrations

## Place Mats

A place for everything and everything in its place—setting the table could not be easier with pockets to hold silverware and napkins. My girls fight over the chance to set the table for me. Okay, in an alternate universe they might but I can dream, can't I?

### Supplies

Makes 2 placemats
- ½ yard background fabric
- ½ yard pocket fabric
- ½ yard backing fabric
- 18" x 40" batting
- 1⅞ yards ½" rickrack
- 3½ yards double-fold bias binding. See pages 75–77 to make yours home sewn.
- Fabric marking pen
- Thread to match
- Rotary cutter, ruler, and mat
- Basic sewing supplies

## Construction

Layer the backing fabric, batting, and background fabric to create a sandwich. Quilt the sandwich as desired. I used a medium-size free-motion doodle.

Cut (2) 14" x 18" rectangles from the quilted background fabric.

Cut (2) 14" x 18" rectangles from the pocket fabric.

Fold the pocket rectangles in half lengthwise with wrong sides together and press. The folded pockets should measure 7" x 18".

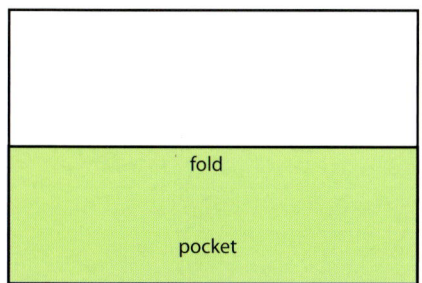

Diagram for the placement of the pocket on the quilted background

Place the pockets over the quilted background fabrics with the fold across the lengthwise center of the background.

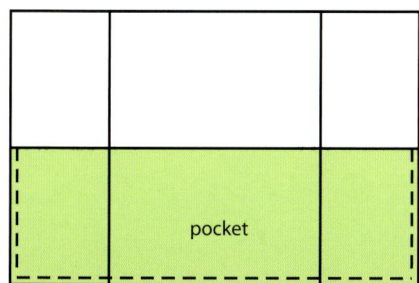

Staystitch the pockets to the quilted background.

Staystitch the sides and bottom of the pockets ⅛" from the outer edges while basting it to the quilted background.

With a ruler measure 5" from left and right sides of the placemat and mark these lines with the fabric marker.

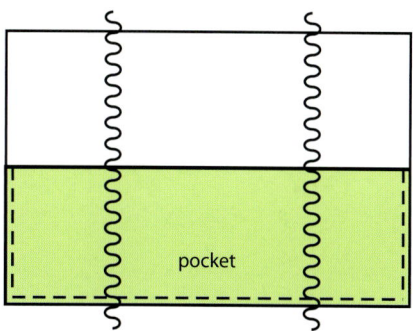

Diagram for the rickrack placement

Cut 4 pieces of rickrack 16" long and place on the drawn lines. Carefully pin in place.

Sew down center of the rickrack with matching thread. Take the pins out just before you stitch to them.

Trim off excess rickrack.

Sew the double-fold bias binding to the edge of the placemat.

Now go set a pretty table!

Garden Party Celebrations

## Napkins

Cloth napkins just make me happy. I believe they make any food-related event a little bit more special. They can be sewn using your favorite fabrics for any occasion or season, are easily laundered, and are a great way to alleviate a little of our carbon footprint. In our home we prefer a large napkin. The measurements below can easily be altered to make any size you desire.

### Supplies

Makes (1) 14" x 14" napkin
- ½ yard fabric
- 1⅔ yards of rickrack, piping, or other trim
- Thread
- Rotary cutter, ruler, and mat
- Basic sewing supplies

### Construction

Cut (2) 14½" x 14½" squares.

Baste the trim to the edges of the right side of one 14½" x 14½" square with a ⅛" seam. Make sure the decorative edge of the trim is toward the body of the napkin. See Tips and Techniques on page 74 for information on attaching rickrack.

Place the squares right sides together. Sew the edges with a ¼" seam allowance leaving a 2" opening.

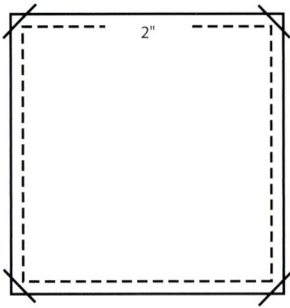

Diagram for sewing and clipping the corners of the napkin

Clip excess fabric from corners and turn inside out. Press.

Topstitch the edges with ⅛" seam.

Tuck onto the nearest lap or under a chin.

Garden Party Celebrations

# Round Casserole Carrier

This round casserole carrier is so cute I have been known to use it and not even leave the house. It's perfect for keeping hot bowls hot and cold bowls cold while picnicking or potlucking. Sewn from fabric matching that favorite sports team and you are ready to tailgate!

## Supplies

- 18" x 18" square of fabric for the top
- ⅔ yard of fabric for the bottom and the handles
- 1 yard of backing fabric
- (2) 18" x 18" squares of batting
- (1) 18" x 24" rectangle of batting
- (2) 18" x 18" squares of Insul~Bright
- (1) 18" x 24" rectangle of Insul~Bright
- 4⅝ yards double-fold bias binding. See pages 75–77 to make yours home sewn.
- 1½ yards of thin round cording or ¼" ribbon
- Basic sewing supplies

Teri Henderson Tope  Home Sewn Celebrations

Garden Party Celebrations

**Full Size Patterns Needed From CD**

28—Round Casserole Carrier Half-Circular Top – Left
29—Round Casserole Carrier Half-Circular Top – Right
30—Round Casserole Carrier Bottom
31—Round Casserole Carrier Handle – Left
32—Round Casserole Carrier Handle – Right

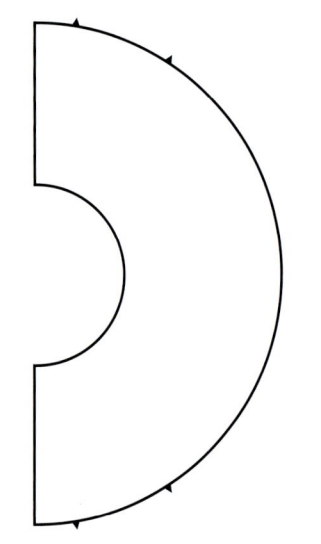

29—Round Casserole Carrier Half-Circular Top – Right

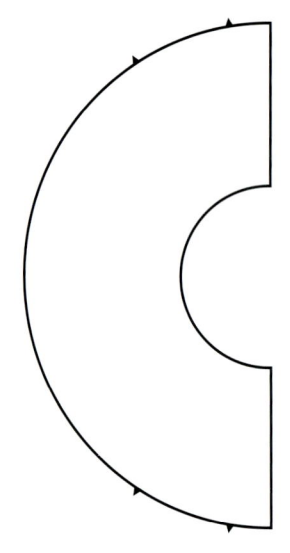

28—Round Casserole Carrier Half-Circular Top – Left

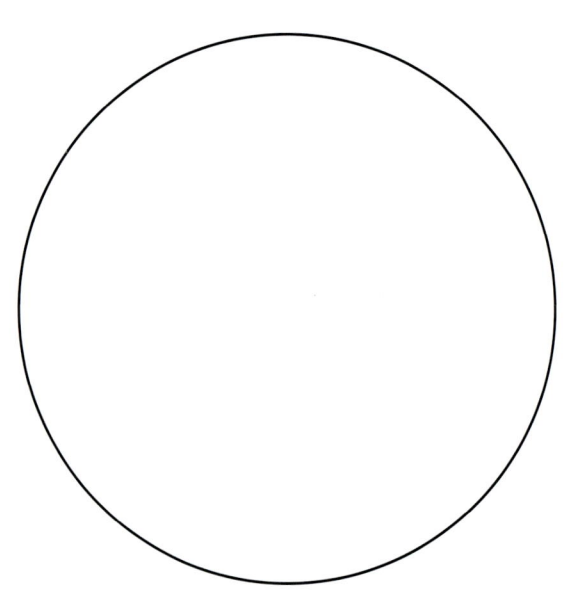

30—Round Casserole Carrier Bottom

Teri Henderson Tope   Home Sewn Celebrations

Garden Party Celebrations

31—Round Casserole Carrier Handle – Left

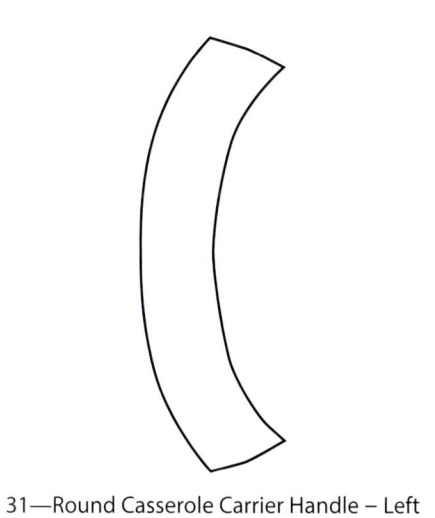

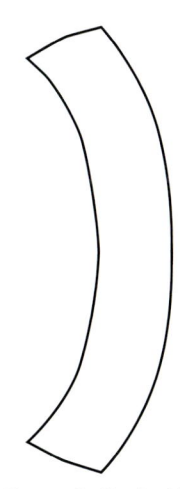

32—Round Casserole Carrier Handle – Right

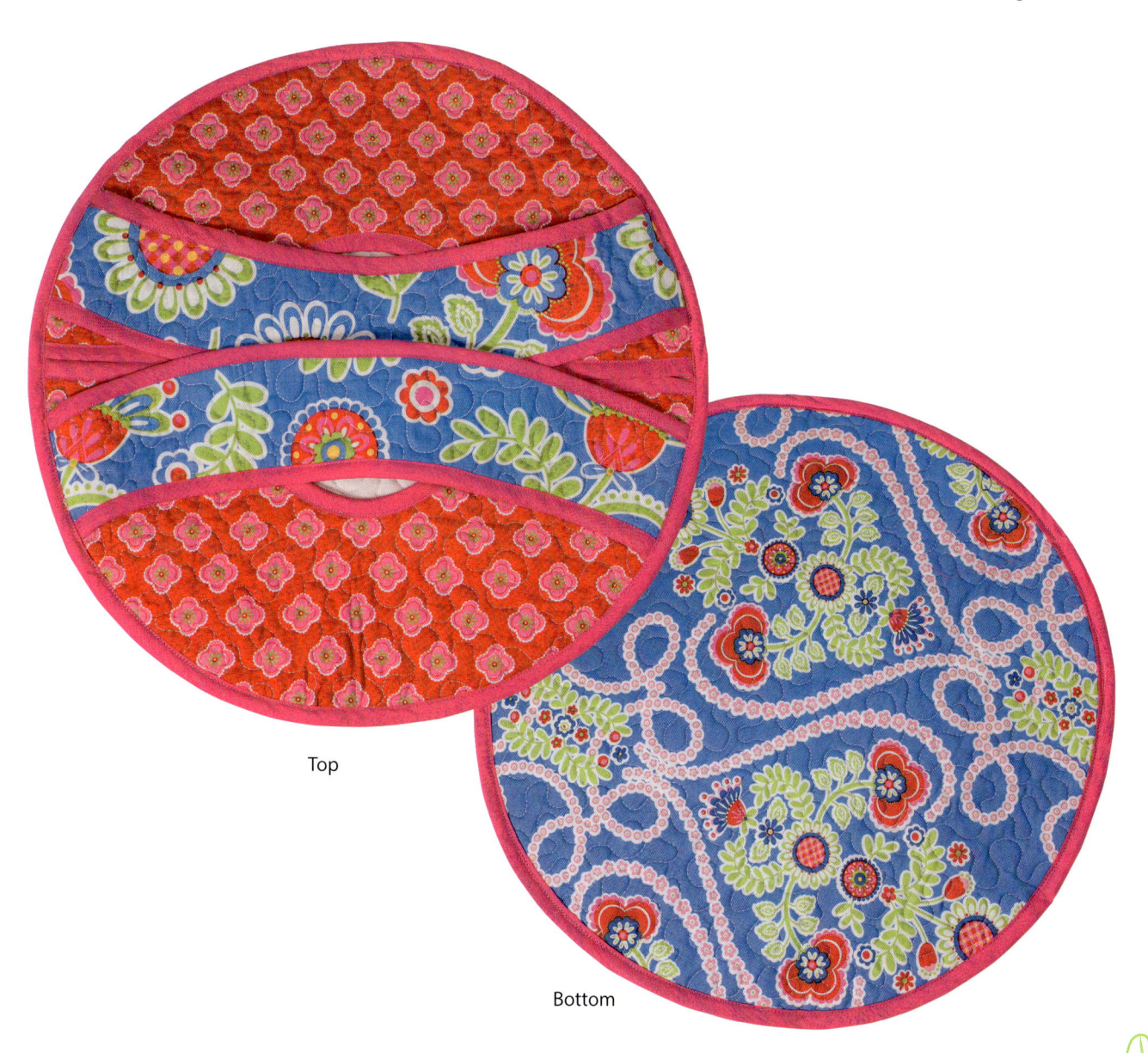

Top

Bottom

Teri Henderson Tope   Home Sewn Celebrations

Garden Party Celebrations

## Construction

From the fabric for the top, cut (1) 18" x 18" square.

From the fabric for the bottom and the handles, cut (1) 18" x 18" square and (1) 18" x 24" rectangle.

From the backing fabric, cut (2) 18" x 18" squares and (1) 18" x 24" rectangle.

On a flat surface, place the 2 backing squares and the backing rectangle face down in a row. On top of them, place first the Insul~Bright squares and rectangle followed by the batting squares and rectangle. On top of the batting, place the fabric squares and rectangle for the top, bottom, and handles face up to create 2 square quilt sandwiches and 1 rectangular quilt sandwich.

Baste the squares and the rectangle. Quilt as desired. My casserole carrier was quilted with a large meander pattern.

Pin the half-circular top left and right patterns on the 18" x 18" quilt sandwich with the fabric for the top facing up. Cut 1 of each.

Pin the circular bottom pattern on the 18" x 18" quilt sandwich with the fabric for the bottom and cut 1 piece.

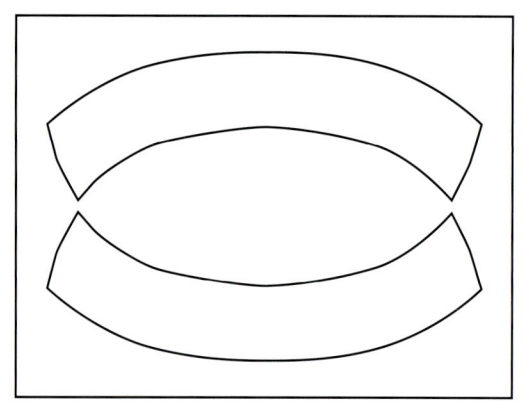

Pattern placement for cutting 2 handles

Pin the handle left and right patterns on the 18" x 24" quilt sandwich and cut 1 of each.

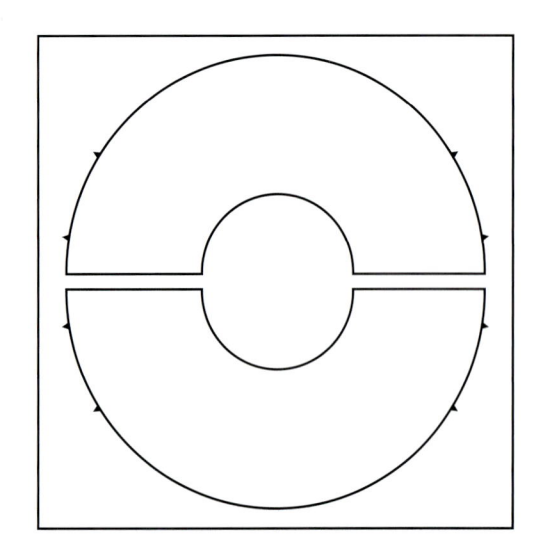

Pattern placement for cutting 2 half-circular top pieces

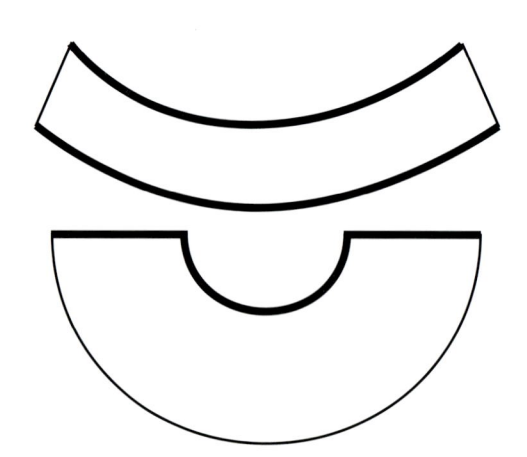

Bind the handles and the short edges of the top pieces.

Teri Henderson Tope   Home Sewn Celebrations

Sew bias binding onto the long edges of both handles and the short ends of both top pieces.

Measure the center curve of the top pieces and add 1" to this measurement. Cut 2 pieces of bias binding to this measurement.

Unfold the bias binding and press a ½" fold on each end of the binding. Stitch ⅛" from the raw edge of the fold to keep it flat. This will create a finished end to the bias binding and, once sewn to the center curve, it will create a casing for the cording or ribbon.

Press the double folds back into the end of the bias binding and stitch to center curve to finish it. Be careful to leave the ends of the bias binding open.

Cut the cording or ribbon in half. Place a knot at each end of the 2 pieces to control raveling.

Insert the cord or ribbon through the casing on each side of the curved center top of the carrier.

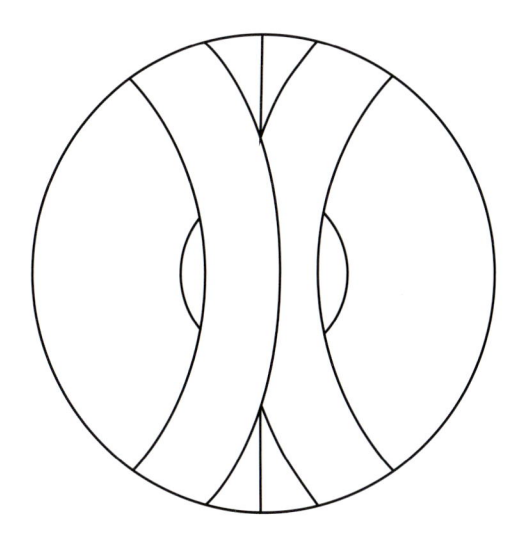

Round casserole carrier assembly diagram

Place the bottom of the carrier on a flat surface face down. Place the top pieces face up over the bottom. Place the handles face up over the top pieces between the handle placement notches.

Pin all of the layers together. Baste the edges together. Attach the bias binding all the way around the outside edge of the carrier.

Put a casserole in the carrier and go to a party!

# Retro Mama Celebrations

This collection of kitchen kitsch was designed with my daughter Andréa in mind. Her sense of style has always weighed in on the side of vintage/retro. A new wife and mother, she uses these items and has given them as gifts to her friends. A much better cook than me, Andréa and her husband entertain often and she is always creating something new and delicious. As her mom, I keep her looking good in the process.

# Retro Mama Apron

Being a modern woman and being the size of a modern woman, I was amazed at the tiny sizes of the vintage aprons my friend Joann collects. Did these ladies not eat? Or is the only reason they are still around is because they were never used? Regardless, I designed this apron so I could wear it and so I could make it with the beautiful fabric I love to sew. Made to easily fit over the head and tied either in front or back, you can quickly stitch a few of these cute aprons for any occasion.

## Supplies

- 1 yard fabric for the front and neck
- ¾ yard fabric for the sides and ties
- (1) fat quarter for the pocket
- 2⅛ yards Lazy Girl Designs Face-It Soft or Pellon Shape-Flex lightweight woven 100% cotton fusible interfacing for the apron front, sides, and neck
- ½ yard rickrack
- 6 yards of ½" double-fold bias tape. See pages 75–77 to make yours home sewn.
- Thread to match
- Rotary cutter, ruler, and mat
- Basic sewing supplies

Retro Mama Celebrations

**Full Size Patterns Needed From CD**

33—Adult Over-The-Head Apron Front
34—Adult Over-The-Head Apron Neck
35—Adult Over-The-Head Apron Side
36—Adult Over-The-Head Pocket
18—Adult Apron Waistband Tie

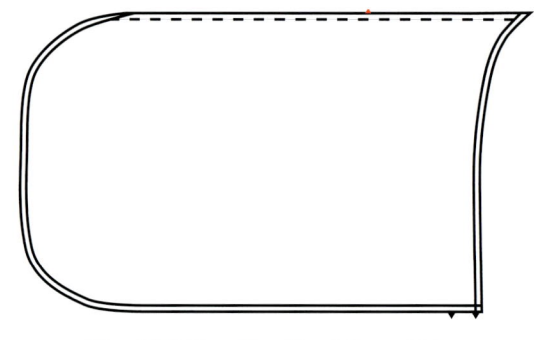

35—Adult Over-The-Head Apron Side

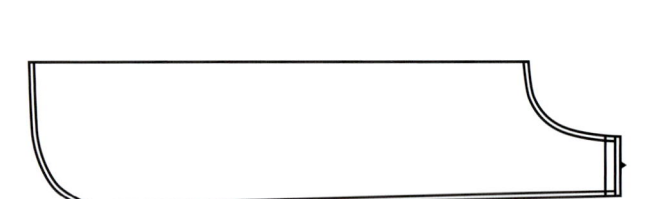

33—Adult Over-The-Head Apron Front

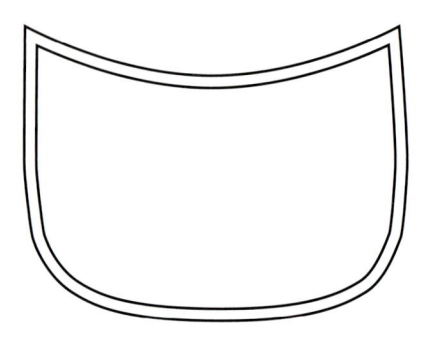

36—Adult Over-The-Head Pocket

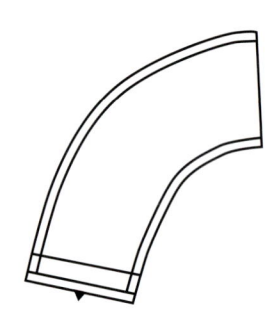

34—Adult Over-The-Head Apron Neck

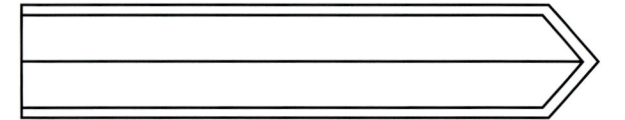

18—Adult Apron Waistband Tie pattern

Teri Henderson Tope    Home Sewn Celebrations

Retro Mama Celebrations

## Construction

Pin the apron front, side, and neck patterns to the woven cotton interfacing and roughly cut them out. The apron front and neck are cut on the fold. Using the side pattern, cut a left side, then turn the pattern over and cut a right side. Following the manufacturer's instructions, fuse the woven cotton interfacing pieces to the wrong side of the apron fabrics. Let them cool.

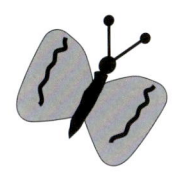

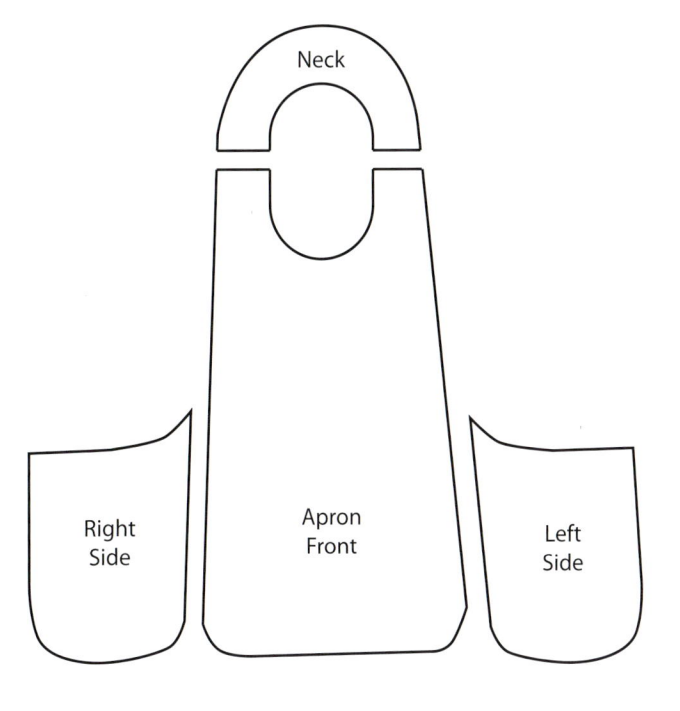

## TIP

Quilter's cotton is a little too lightweight for apron purposes. To reinforce the fabric, iron lightweight woven 100% cotton fusible interfacing to the wrong side of the front, side, and neck fabrics.

Teri Henderson Tope • Home Sewn Celebrations

45

## Retro Mama Celebrations

Sew bias binding to the top, bottom, and outer side (not the inner side) of the right and left side pieces.

The apron neck is sewn together with a French seam. See page 75 for information on a French seam. With wrong sides together, sew the neck to the top of the apron front using a ¼" seam allowance. Press the seam to one side.

Fold the neck and apron front at the seam with right sides together and press.

Sew a ½" seam capturing the previously sewn ¼" seam allowance inside. Press towards the neck.

Sew bias binding around the inside of the neck.

Sew the right and left sides to the apron front, wrong sides together, using a ¼" seam allowance matching notches.

Sew bias binding around the apron front, catching the left and right sides. Press the bias binding flat over the sides and topstitch close to the edge.

Sew 2 pocket pieces right sides together, leaving a 2" opening. Repeat with the 2 remaining pocket pieces.

Clip the corners and curves, then turn the pockets inside out and press.

Attach the rickrack to the pocket fronts 1" from the top of the pocket. See Tips and Techniques on page 74 for information on attaching rickrack.

Pin the pockets to the apron and stitch ⅛" around the edges of the sides and bottom of the pocket. Topstitch again ¼" from the edges.

Fold the waistband ties lengthwise with right sides together. Sew the ties together leaving the straight end open. Turn them inside out and press. Press a small pleat on the open end of the apron tie as indicated on the pattern.

Place the raw edge of the tie end ⅛" from the edge on the back of the apron side at the position shown on the pattern.

Securely attach the tie ends to the apron using the stitching pattern below while encasing the folded raw edges of the ties between the apron and the tie.

Detail of binding on the front and sides of the apron

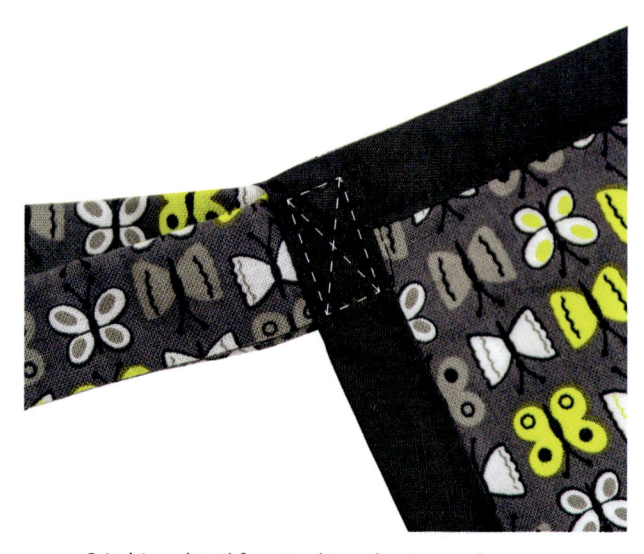

Stitching detail for attaching the ties to the apron

Teri Henderson Tope  Home Sewn Celebrations

Retro Mama Celebrations

Completed apron

This is a great gift for a cook in your life, especially if they will do some cooking for you!

Teri Henderson Tope  Home Sewn Celebrations

Retro Mama Celebrations

# Rectangular Casserole Carrier

Many years ago, I was given a newspaper pattern of this casserole carrier by a member of the Grace United Church circle, Threads of Grace, in Gallipolis, Ohio. Used over and over, it has always been a potluck favorite. My trick? Pick up something yummy at the grocery store and pop it into a 9" x 13" casserole dish. Tuck it into this lovely casserole carrier and you will be the hit of the party. Works every time!

## Supplies

- ¾ yard fabric for the top
- ¾ yard fabric for the backing
- 24" x 40" batting
- (1) 5/16" dowel rod cut into (2) 12½" pieces
- 6" of Velcro Hook and Loop fastener tape
- 8½" x 12" piece of heavy cardboard
- 6½ yards of double-fold bias binding. See pages 75–77 to make yours home sewn.
- Thread to match
- Rotary cutter, ruler, and mat
- Basic sewing supplies

## Full Size Patterns Needed From CD

37—Rectangular Casserole Carrier Rounded Corner Section

38—Rectangular Casserole Carrier Handle Section

37—Rectangular Casserole Carrier Rounded Corner Section

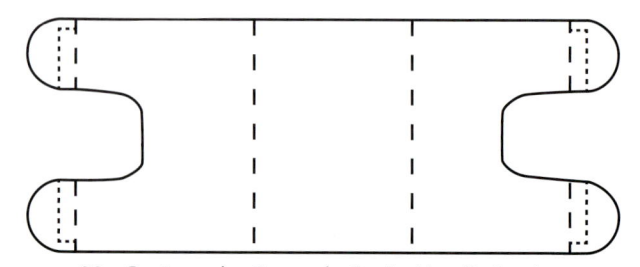

38—Rectangular Casserole Carrier Handle Section

48     Teri Henderson Tope   Home Sewn Celebrations

Retro Mama Celebrations

## Construction

Make a sandwich of the top fabric, batting, and backing fabric. Quilt as desired. I outline quilted around the fabric print motifs.

Pin the patterns onto the quilted fabric and cut them out.

Attach bias binding to the outside edges of both pieces.

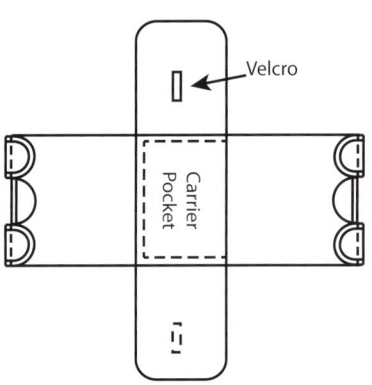

Final assembly diagram

Dowel rod pocket diagram

Fold the handle ends, backing sides together, at the marks on the pattern. Sew along stitching lines to create pockets for the dowel rods.

Insert the dowel rods into the pockets.

Place the handle section face down. Perpendicularly center the smaller rounded corner piece face down over the handle.

Stitch the three sides indicated on the illustration above to create a carrier pocket for the cardboard and to attach the two quilted pieces together.

Sew Velcro onto the flaps of carrier as shown above.

Insert the cardboard into the carrier pocket.

Go to the picnic in style!

Teri Henderson Tope · Home Sewn Celebrations

49

Retro Mama Celebrations

# Oven Mitt

I never seem to be able to find these pot holders when I need one. They are so cute that they disappear as quickly as I make them. I suspect my daughters have them hidden in their hope chests. So stitch up a few for yourself and brighten your kitchen while you are at it.

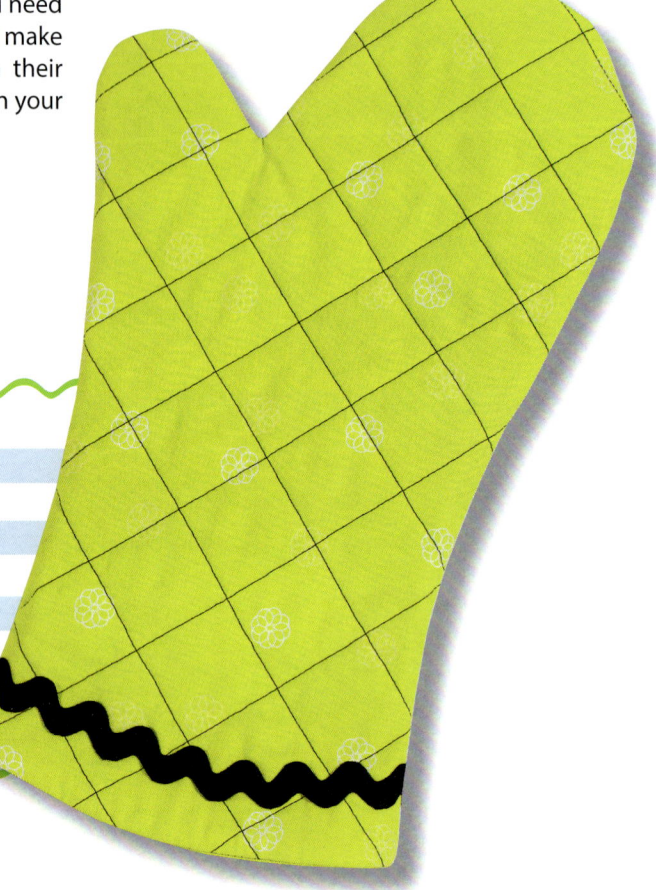

## Supplies

Makes 2 oven mitts
- ½ yard fabric for the oven mitt top
- ½ yard fabric for the oven mitt backing
- 1" x 27" strip of fabric for the inside facings
- 18" x 40" piece of Insul~Bright
- 18" x 40" piece of batting
- 1 yard ½" rickrack
- Thread to match
- Basic sewing supplies

## Full Size Pattern Needed From the CD

39—Oven Mitt

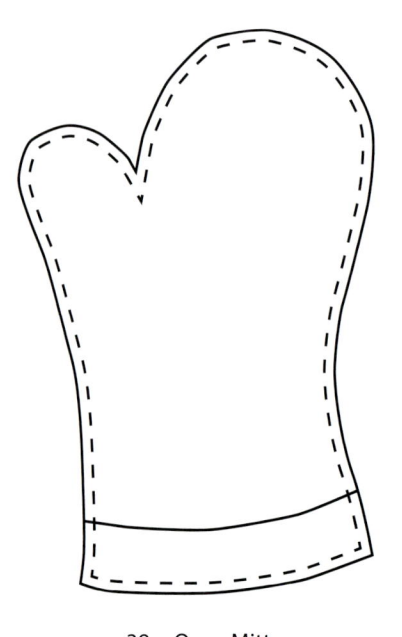

39—Oven Mitt

Teri Henderson Tope   Home Sewn Celebrations

## Construction

Place the backing fabric face down. Layer the batting and then the Insul~Bright on the backing. Place the mitt top fabric right-side up on the stack to make a quilt sandwich.

Baste and quilt as desired. My oven mitt is quilted in a cross-hatch design.

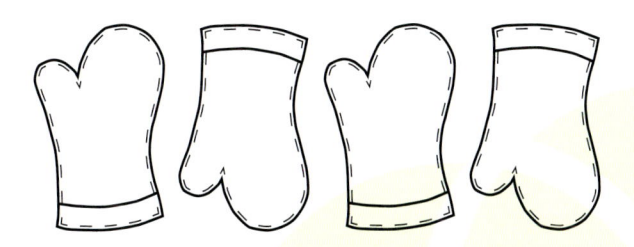

Oven mitt cutting diagram

Using oven mitt pattern, cut 2 right hand mitts and 2 left hand mitts from the quilted fabric, referring to the cutting diagram above.

Sew the rickrack to the mitts 1½" from the raw edge along the line shown on the patterns.

Pin a left mitt to a right mitt with right sides together and sew a ¼" seam around outside edge as shown on the pattern. Stitch the seam twice to ensure that it does not come undone. Finish the edge of this seam with a zigzag stitch.

Carefully clip the curve inside the thumb of the oven mitt. If the stitching is even slightly nicked, resew the seam. You will thank me later.

Repeat the two previous steps to make the second mitt.

Turn the oven mitts inside out and press.

For the inside facings, cut the 1" x 27" strip of fabric in half to make (2) 1" x 13½" facings.

Stitch the short ends of the facings right sides together with a ¼" seam to form circles. Press the seams open.

Press a ¼" fold wrong sides together on one side of each facing.

Pin the unfolded edges of the facings to the oven mitts with right sides together and stitch together with a ¼" seam.

Fold the facings along the seam lines toward the insides of the mitts and stitch them down by hand or machine.

We are ready to cook now! Let's go bake some cookies!

Retro Mama Celebrations

## Hanging Kitchen Towel

I am sure we have all owned numerous versions of this hanging kitchen towel. I combined all my favorites to design this pattern. I think they just make the oven door look finished. Easily switched for every season, they are often one of the first items I decorate with. They also are a great apartment or housewarming gift. I have even made a baseball-themed set for a favorite nephew. Got to love a novelty print!

### Supplies

Makes 1 towel
- 1 fat quarter
- ½ yard Lazy Girl Designs Face-It Soft or Pellon Shape-Flex lightweight woven 100% cotton fusible interfacing
- Kitchen towel, dish cloth, or tea towel
- Decorative trim 2" longer than the width of the towel
- Decorative button
- ½" x 2" piece of Velcro Hook and Loop fastener
- Thread to match fabric
- Sewing machine with walking foot
- Pinking shears
- Rotary cutter, ruler, and mat
- Basic sewing supplies

## Full Size Pattern Needed From the CD

40—Hanging Kitchen Towel

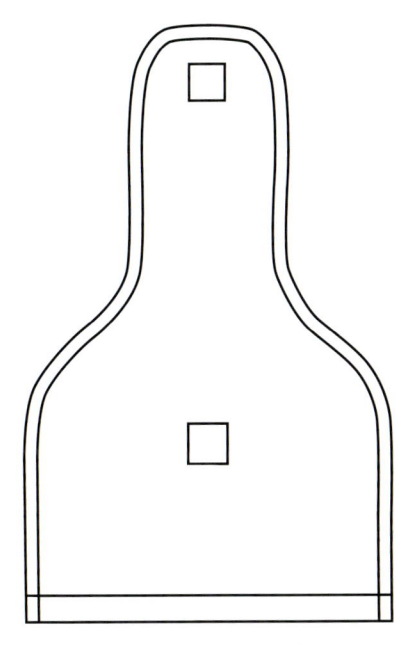

40—Hanging Kitchen Towel pattern

## Construction

With a ruler and rotary cutter, trim the top hem off of the dish cloth or tea towel to eliminate excess bulk.

Sew a basting stitch across the trimmed top ¼" from the raw edge and gather the towel to 6½".

Fuse the interfacing to the back of the fat quarter.

Fold the fat quarter in half. Pin the hanging towel pattern to the fabric and cut 2 pieces.

With right sides together sew a ¼" seam around the hanger top leaving the bottom edge open.

Using pinking shears, trim the curved edges.

Turn the hanger right-side out and press.

Press a ½" hem along the bottom edge of the hanger.

Insert the gathered towel into the hanger. Baste the layers together with needle and thread.

On a sewing machine, topstitch ¼" around the edge of the hanger and across the bottom where the towel is sandwiched. For extra support, sew a ⅛" seam across the bottom close to the towel.

Using the pattern, mark the placement of the Velcro and securely stitch it into place.

Attach a decorative button over the Velcro on the end of the flap.

Measure the bottom edge of the towel. Add two inches to this measurement and cut a piece of trim to this length. With a clear ruler, measure 1½" from the bottom of the towel and pin the trim evenly across it with 1" of trim extending beyond each edge. With the sewing machine, sew the trim into place. Tuck the trim ends to the back and hand stitch to secure them.

# Tailgate Celebrations

Okay, being from Ohio, living in a suburb of Columbus, married to an Ohio State graduate, and having raised two Ohio State University graduates, I might just know a thing or two about tailgating at a football game. Many a fall Saturday afternoon, our family can be found down at the Shoe or camped out in front of the TV cheering on our Buckeyes! There is nothing like a Buckeye fan and there is nothing like the atmosphere at an Ohio State football game. We have taken tailgating to extreme measures.

# Tailgate Apron—Adult

In honor of all our wonderful sports teams, I have created this fun little apron that could also double as a Halloween costume.

## Supplies

- 1¼ yards fabric for bib, neck, skirt, waistband, and ties
- ¼ yard or a fat quarter for skirt inserts
- 1 yard of Lazy Girl Designs Face-It Soft or Pellon Shape-Flex lightweight woven 100% cotton fusible interfacing for the bib and neck
- 4" x 6" piece of lightweight fusible web (for optional bib appliqué)
- 4" x 6" piece of fabric (for optional bib appliqué)
- 3 yards of ½" rickrack
- Thread to match
- 6" x 24" ruler
- Rotary cutter, ruler, and mat
- Basic sewing supplies

Tailgate Celebrations

## Full Size Patterns Needed From CD

41—Apron Bodice Bib – Adult
42—Apron Bodice Neck – Adult
43—Apron Pleated Front Skirt A – Adult
44—Apron Pleated Side Skirt B Left – Adult
45—Apron Pleated Side Skirt B Right – Adult
46—Apron Pleated Skirt Insert – Adult
47—Apron Pleated Skirt Waistband – Adult
18—Adult Apron Waistband Tie

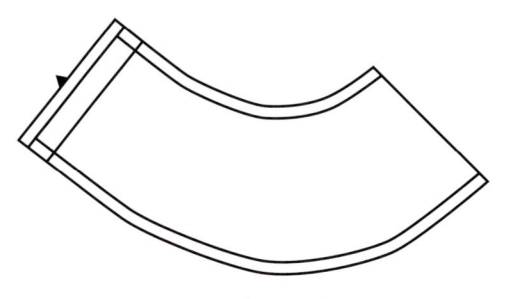

42—Apron Bodice Neck – Adult

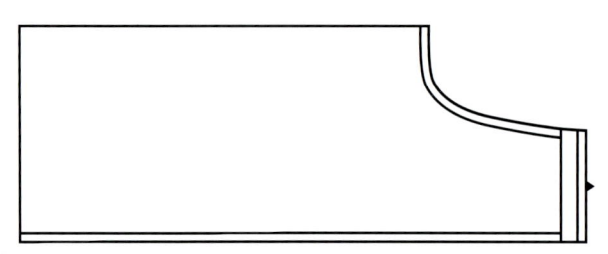

41—Apron Bodice Bib – Adult

43—Apron Pleated Front Skirt A – Adult

44—Apron Pleated Side Skirt B Left – Adult

Teri Henderson Tope   Home Sewn Celebrations

Tailgate Celebrations

45—Apron Pleated Side Skirt B Right – Adult

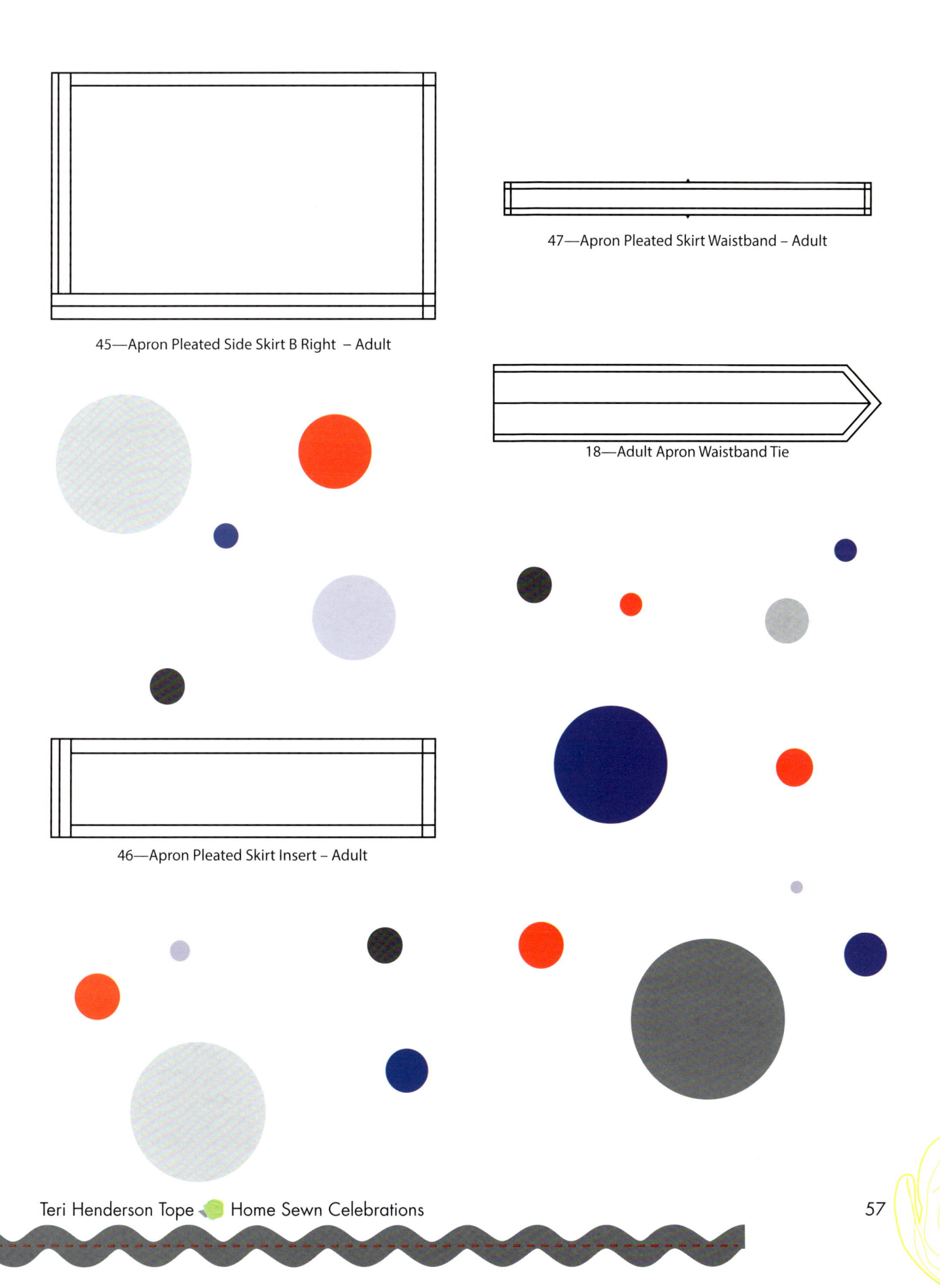

47—Apron Pleated Skirt Waistband – Adult

18—Adult Apron Waistband Tie

46—Apron Pleated Skirt Insert – Adult

Teri Henderson Tope  Home Sewn Celebrations

57

Tailgate Celebrations

## Construction

Roughly cut out enough lightweight woven 100% cotton fusible interfacing to line the bib and neck pattern pieces and fuse it to the back of the bib and neck fabric. Pin the pattern pieces to the interfaced fabric and cut them out.

Pin remaining tailgate apron pattern pieces to the appropriate fabrics and cut them out.

### Bib

The shoulder seam is a French seam. See page 75 for information about French seams. Place the neck and bib pieces wrong sides together. Pin at the shoulder seam and sew with a ¼" seam. Press to one side.

Fold the shoulder seam right sides together, capturing the ¼" seam allowance in the fold. Sew a ½" seam. Press the seam away from the bodice.

Attach rickrack to the raw edges of the bib's sides and neck opening. See Tips and Techniques on page 74 for information on attaching rickrack.

Optional: Trace a letter on the wrong side of the fusible web. Remember to trace the letter in reverse so that it will be in the correct direction when attached.

Fuse the web to the back of the appliqué fabric and cut the letter out. Press and fuse it to the front of the apron bib.

With a zigzag stitch, cover the raw edge of the appliqué.

### Pleated Skirt

The Side Skirt B pieces need a finished side edge—the right side edge for the right side skirt and the left side edge for the left side skirt. Press a ¼" fold along these side edges, then make a ½" fold and press again. Sew along the fold to the finish edge.

Teri Henderson Tope  Home Sewn Celebrations

Tailgate Celebrations

In order to have the pleats hang correctly you will need to hem the bottom of each piece before sewing them together. With an iron press a ¼" fold on the bottom of all of the skirt pieces. Then make a ½" fold and press. Sew along folded edge to create a hem on each piece.

On a flat surface lay out the skirt pieces as follows from left to right:
Side Skirt B Right
Skirt Insert 1
Front Skirt A 1
Skirt Insert 2
Front Skirt A 2
Skirt Insert 3
Front Skirt A 3
Skirt Insert 4
Side Skirt B Left

Sew the pieces together with a ½" seam allowance. Do not press yet.

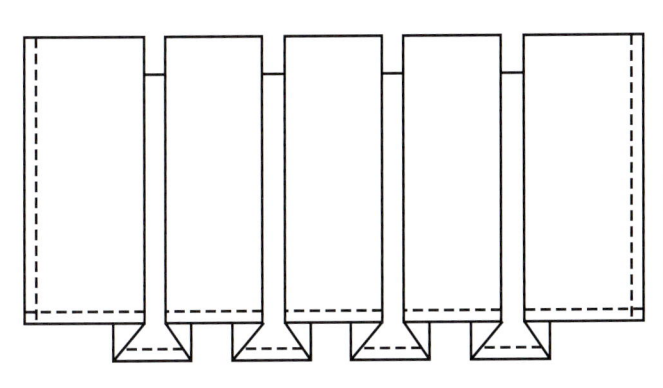

Pleated skirt assembly diagram

We are now going to make the pleats.

With a ruler, find the vertical center of Skirt Insert 1. Keeping Skirt Insert 1 flat, carefully fold Side Skirt B Right to the center of the insert. Pin and press the fold.

Now fold Front Skirt A1 over Skirt Insert 1 meeting the fold from Side Skirt B Right to completely cover Skirt Insert 1. Pin and press.

With a ruler find the vertical center of Skirt Insert 2. Keeping Skirt Insert 2 flat, carefully fold Front Skirt A 1 to the center of Insert 2. Pin and press the fold.

Now fold Front Skirt A2 over Skirt Insert 2 meeting the fold from Front Skirt A1 to completely cover Insert 2. Pin and press.

Continue this folding and pleating process for all of the remaining skirt pieces as shown in the diagram on the left.

Staystitch ¼" along the top edge of the skirt, encompassing all of the pleats as you stitch.

Press a ½" fold along the bottom edge of the waistband.

On a flat surface, place the pleated skirt right-side down. Place the bib over the skirt matching the raw edges with wrong sides together.

Place the waistband over the bib right sides together matching raw edges. Pin and sew a ½" seam through all layers.

Fold the apron ties in half lengthwise and, with right sides together, sew a ½" seam allowance leaving the straight end unsewn. Trim the corners. Pull the ties right-side out. Turn inside out and press.

Place the unfinished end of the tie right sides together over the waistband making a small pleat to make it fit within the tie guidelines. Sew the tie to the waistband using a ½" seam allowance.

Flip the waistband down and top stitch to securely attach. Press.

Teri Henderson Tope — Home Sewn Celebrations

Tailgate Celebrations

# Tailgate Apron—Child

The child's tailgate apron is constructed the same as the adult's. Below are the supplies and patterns needed for this smaller size. Use the instructions for the adult's apron beginning on page 55.

## Supplies

- 1⅛ yards fabric for bib, neck, skirt, waistband, and ties
- ¼ yard or a fat quarter for skirt inserts
- ⅔ yard of Lazy Girl Designs Face-It Soft or Pellon Shape-Flex lightweight woven 100% cotton fusible interfacing for the bib and neck
- 4" x 6" piece of lightweight fusible web (for optional bib appliqué)
- 4" x 6" piece of fabric (for optional bib appliqué)
- 2 yards of ½" rickrack
- Thread to match
- 6" x 24" ruler
- Rotary cutter, ruler, and mat
- Basic sewing supplies

Teri Henderson Tope — Home Sewn Celebrations

Tailgate Celebrations

## Full Size Patterns Needed From CD

48—Apron Bodice Bib – Child
49—Apron Bodice Neck – Child
50—Apron Pleated Front Skirt A – Child
51—Apron Pleated Side Skirt B Left – Child
52—Apron Pleated Side Skirt B Right – Child
53—Apron Pleated Skirt Insert – Child
54—Apron Pleated Skirt Waistband – Child
25—Child Apron Waistband Tie

50—Apron Pleated Front Skirt A – Child

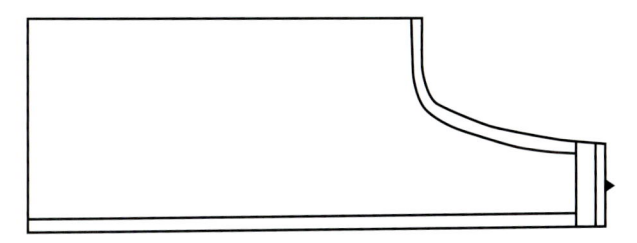

48—Apron Bodice Bib – Child

51—Apron Pleated Side Skirt B Left – Child

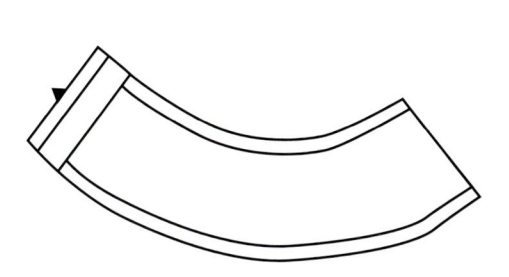

49—Apron Bodice Neck – Child

Teri Henderson Tope   Home Sewn Celebrations

Tailgate Celebrations

52—Apron Pleated Side Skirt B Right – Child

54—Apron Pleated Skirt Waistband – Child

53—Apron Pleated Skirt Insert – Child

25—Child Apron Waistband Tie

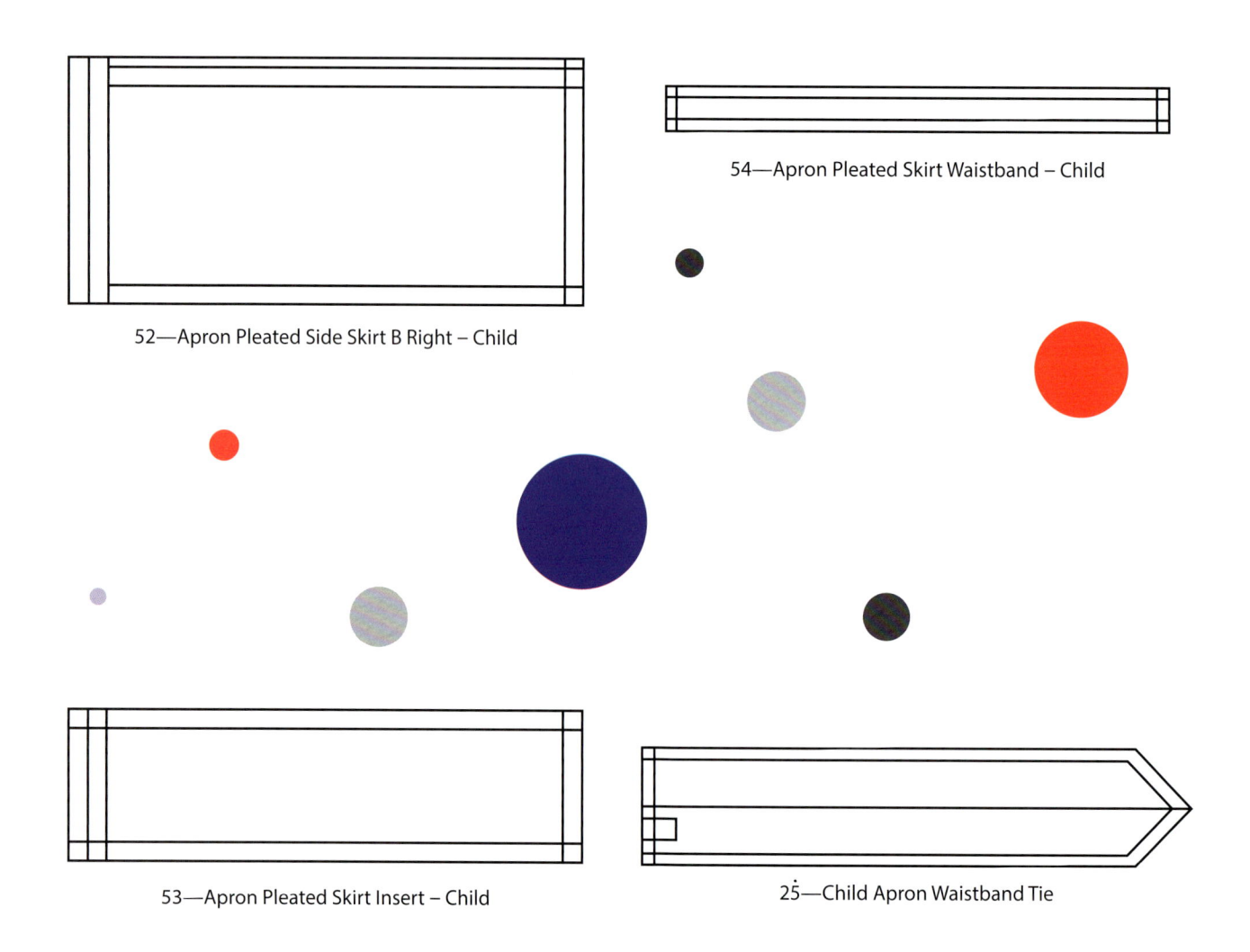

## Construction

Please see the Tailgate Apron – Adult project on pages 55–59 for instructions.

Teri Henderson Tope　Home Sewn Celebrations

Tailgate Celebrations

# Insulated Bottle Carrier

This special little bag contains Insul~Bright which will keep cold things cold and hot things hot. It is also a bit larger than the average bottle bag which makes it easier to carry and to put larger items such as a two liter soda inside. Perfect for that football game or sporting event! Add a little decorative quilting and it makes a great container for any gift.

## Supplies

Makes 1 bottle carrier
- ½ yard exterior fabric
- ½ yard lining fabric
- ½ yard Insul~Bright
- ½ yard double-fold bias binding. See pages 75–77 to make yours home sewn.
- Thread
- Pinking shears
- Sewing machine with walking foot
- Basic sewing supplies

Teri Henderson Tope   Home Sewn Celebrations

63

Tailgate Celebrations

## Full Size Patterns Needed From CD

55—Insulated Bottle Carrier Sides
56—Insulated Bottle Carrier Bottom

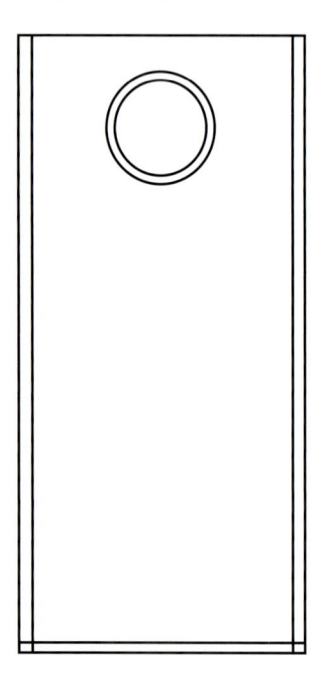

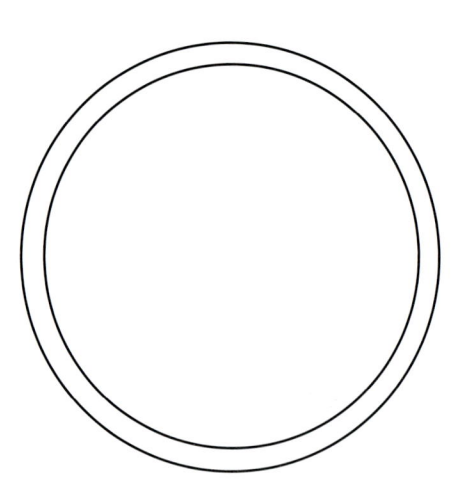

56—Insulated Bottle Carrier Bottom

55—Insulated Bottle Carrier Sides

Teri Henderson Tope • Home Sewn Celebrations

Tailgate Celebrations

## Construction

Cut (2) 8½" x 18" rectangles each from the exterior fabric, lining fabric, and the Insul~Bright for the sides.

Cut (1) 7" x 7" square each from the exterior fabric, lining fabric, and the Insul~Bright for the bottom.

Center the bottle carrier side pattern on the wrong side of the (2) 8½" x 18" lining fabric rectangles. Trace the circular handle at the top of the bag with a fabric-marking tool.

Trace the circular handle on the wrong side of the lining fabric rectangles.

Teri Henderson Tope  Home Sewn Celebrations

65

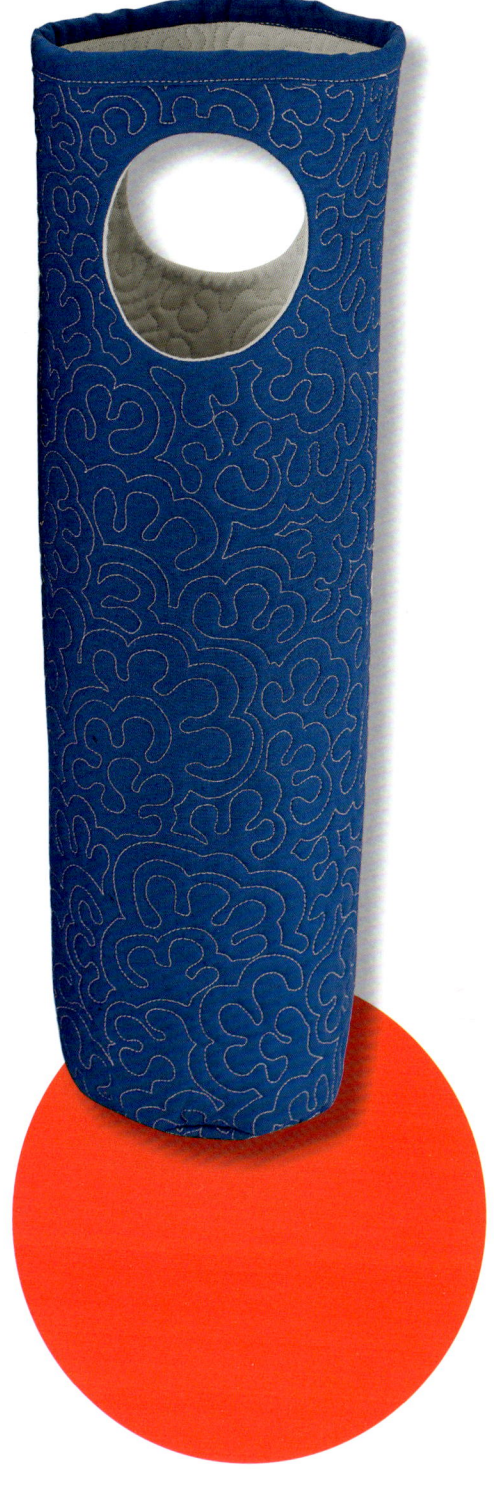

## Tailgate Celebrations

Place the (2) 8½" x 18" side Insul~Bright rectangles on a flat surface. On top of each of them, place an 8½" x 18" side exterior fabric rectangle face up. On top of each of the exterior fabric rectangles, place the 8½" x 18" side lining fabric rectangles face down with the drawn circles showing. Pin all of the layers together.

With a walking foot, sew along the traced line of the circular handle on the bag sides.

Cut out the interior of the circle leaving a ¼" seam allowance. Trim the edges with pinking shears.

Carefully pull the lining fabric through the cut hole and press.

Match all of the edges of the 8½" x 18" side rectangles and pin securely.

Machine quilt the rectangles as desired. Remove the pins as you sew.

Pin the bottle carrier side pattern to the rectangles and cut them out.

Place the 7" x 7" bottom square of exterior fabric face down on a flat surface and then place the 7" x 7" bottom square of Insul~Bright on top of it. Place the 7" x 7" bottom square of lining fabric face up on top of the Insul~Bright. Carefully match the edges and then pin all of the layers together.

Machine quilt the square as desired.

Pin the bottle carrier bottom pattern to the square and cut it out.

Pin the quilted sides right sides together and sew one long edge with a ¼" seam using the walking foot.

Finish the edge with a zigzag stitch. Press the seam to one side.

Staystitch ¼" along the lower edge of the bag. This will help you attach the bag sides to the bottom.

With scissors, clip the lower edge of the bag every ⅛", stopping the clip just before the ¼" sewn line.

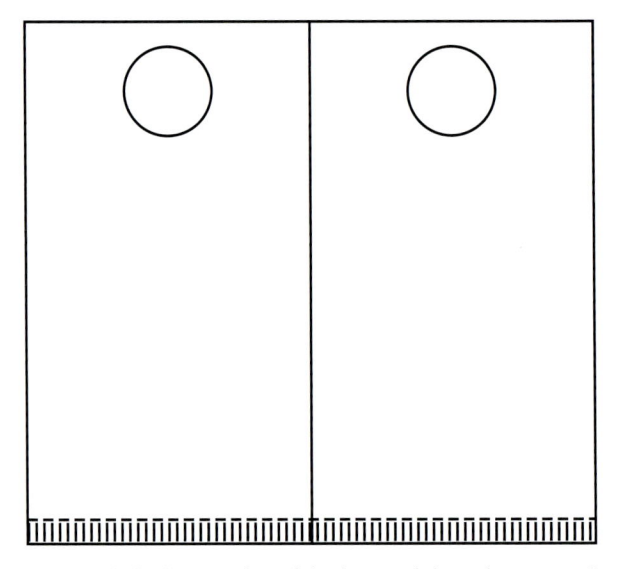

Staystitch the lower edge of the bag and then clip every ⅛".

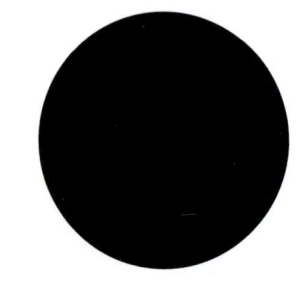

Teri Henderson Tope  Home Sewn Celebrations

Tailgate Celebrations

Place the bag sides right sides together and stitch the remaining side of the bag with a ¼" seam. Finish the seam with a zigzag stitch.

With the bag turned wrong-side out, sew the bag bottom right sides together to the bag sides by first attaching the clipped edge of the bag sides to the bag bottom with a zigzag stitch. Then carefully sew a ¼" seam on the staystitching at the lower edge of the bag sides.

Turn the bag inside out.

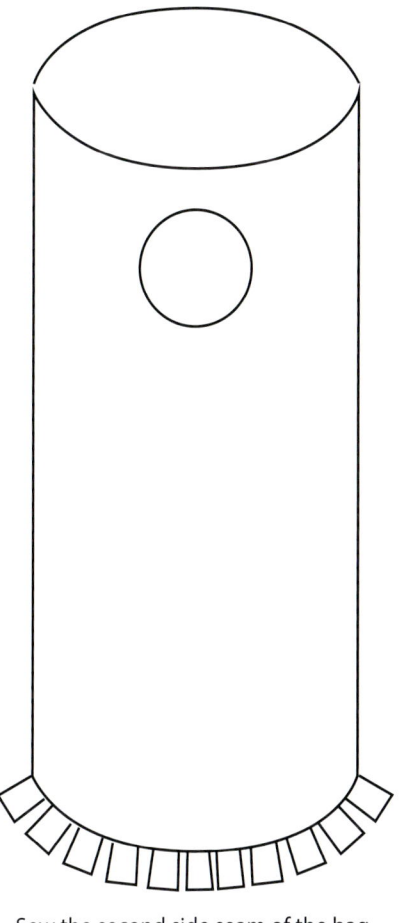

Sew bias binding over the raw edge of the bag top to finish the bag.

Now fill it with your favorite beverage.

Sew the second side seam of the bag.

Teri Henderson Tope 🍏 Home Sewn Celebrations

# Sweetheart Celebration

For any celebration, it is fun to show the loved ones in your life that they are indeed loved. Here is a sweetheart of an apron to give or wear in honor of these special people. This is the easiest apron to construct in this book. I promise you can make this perfect hostess apron in a short amount of time.

Sweetheart Celebration

# Sweetheart Apron

## Supplies

- 1½ yards fabric for the inner skirt, waistband, waistband ties, and heart pocket (shown in red)
- ⅝ yards fabric for the outer skirt (shown in white)
- 1⅛ yards Lazy Girl Designs Face-It Soft or Pellon Shape-Flex lightweight woven 100% cotton fusible interfacing for the inner skirt and waistband
- 2⅛ yards rickrack for the inner skirt
- 1¾ yards rickrack for the outer skirt
- Thread to match
- Basic sewing supplies

Teri Henderson Tope 🌿 Home Sewn Celebrations

Sweetheart Celebration

**Full Size Patterns Needed From CD**
57—Swing Apron Inner Skirt
58—Swing Apron Outer Skirt
59—Swing Apron Waistband
60—Heart Apron Pocket
18—Adult Apron Waistband Tie

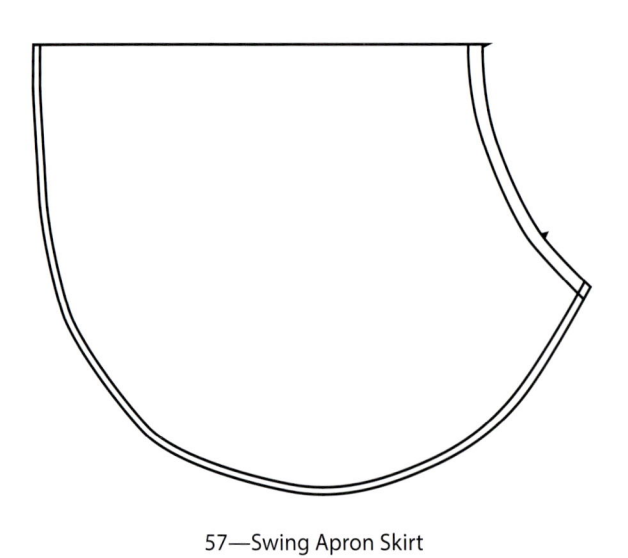

57—Swing Apron Skirt

59—Swing Apron Waistband

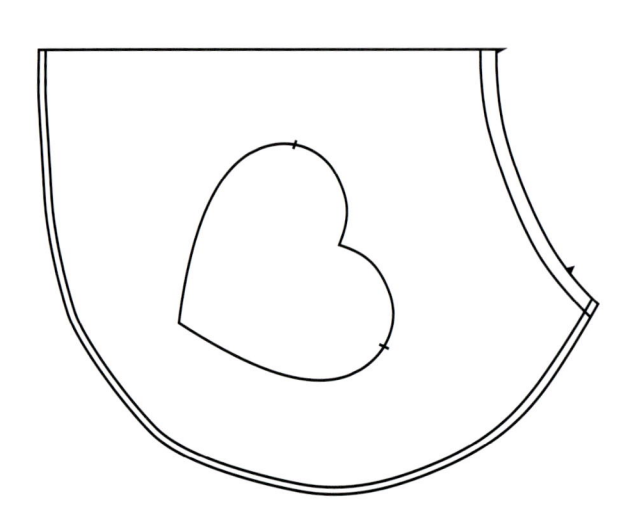

58—Swing Apron Skirt

60—Heart Apron Pocket

18—Adult Swing Apron Waistband Tie

## Construction

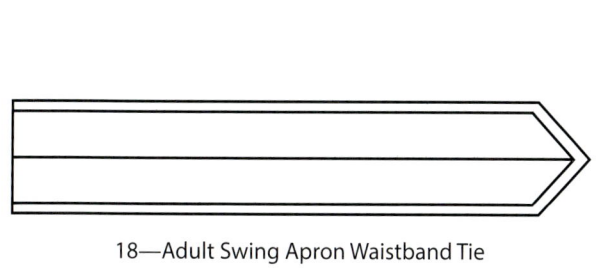

Cut pieces of interfacing larger than the inner skirt and waistband patterns. Fuse them to the appropriate fabric. Pin the patterns for the inner skirt and waistband to the interfaced fabric and cut them out.

Sew rickrack to the outside edges of the inner skirt and the outer skirt. See Tips and Techniques on page 74 for information on attaching rickrack.

Cut 2 heart pockets and place them right sides together. Stitch a ½" seam around the edge of the heart, leaving a 2" opening along one side for turning the pocket inside out. Stitch the inward point at the top of the heart a second time for security. Trim the seam to ¼" with pinking shears. With regular scissors, make a small snip almost to the seam at the inward point at the top of the heart.

Turn the pocket inside out. Roll the seam line gently between your fingers to create a smooth heart-shaped edge and press. Hand stitch the opening of the pocket closed. Topstitch ¼" all the way around the heart pocket.

Position the pocket on the left side of the outer skirt using the pocket placement diagram on the outer skirt pattern. Topstitch the heart pocket a second time between the marks on the pocket pattern, topstitching around the sides and bottom of the heart to attach it to the outer skirt, leaving the top of the pocket unattached.

Layer the outer skirt over the inner skirt and staystitch ¼" along the top edge of the outer skirt. This will stabilize the upper curve of the skirts.

Sweetheart Celebration

Prepare the waistband.

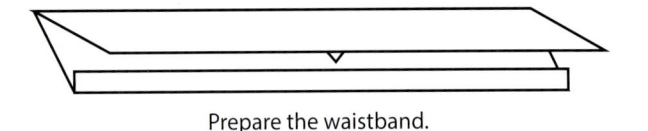

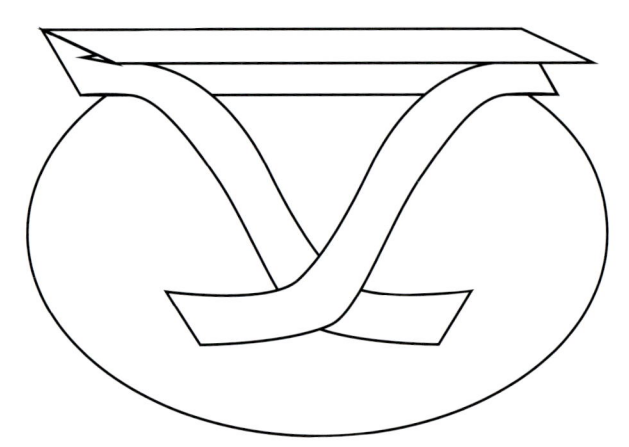

Pin the apron ties to the waistband.

Match the raw edges of the ties with the outer edge of the waistband right sides together and pin. The apron ties will rest on the apron front.

Press the waistband in half with wrong sides together. Press a ½" fold on the unnotched edge of the waistband.

Pin the waistband right sides together with the upper edge of the skirt matching the center notches. Sew them together with a ½" seam allowance.

Fold the skirt ties right sides together and stitch with a ½" seam allowance leaving the straight ends unsewn. Clip the points, turn them inside out, and press.

Make a small pleat at the raw end of each tie to allow it to fit within the width of the waistband. Baste.

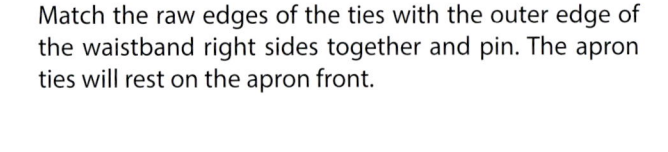

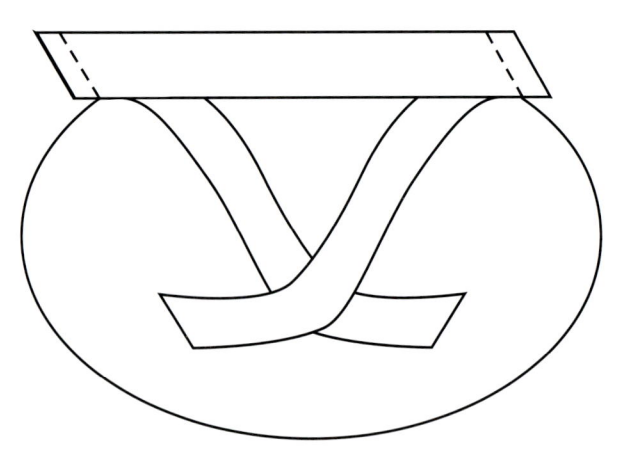

Stitch the waistband and ties.

Fold the waistband over the ties with right sides together. Make sure the ½" fold on the back of the waistband is even with the edge of the skirt. Pin and stitch with a ½" seam. Turn inside out.

Stitch the back of the waistband to the top back edge of the skirt.

You now have an incredibly sweet apron!

Sweetheart Celebration

Teri Henderson Tope — Home Sewn Celebrations

73

# Tips and Techniques

**Rickrack**

Place the rickrack along the edge of the area to be covered. Leave a ½" tail at the beginning and end.

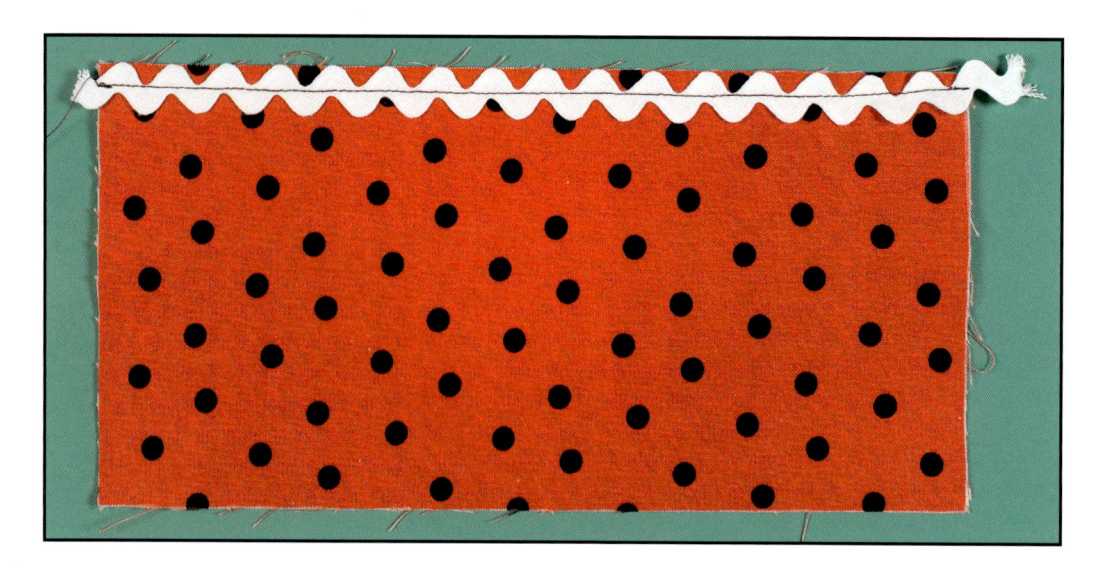

Stitch through the center of the rickrack with a sewing machine.

Fold the raw edge to the inside along the stitched line.

Press with an iron.

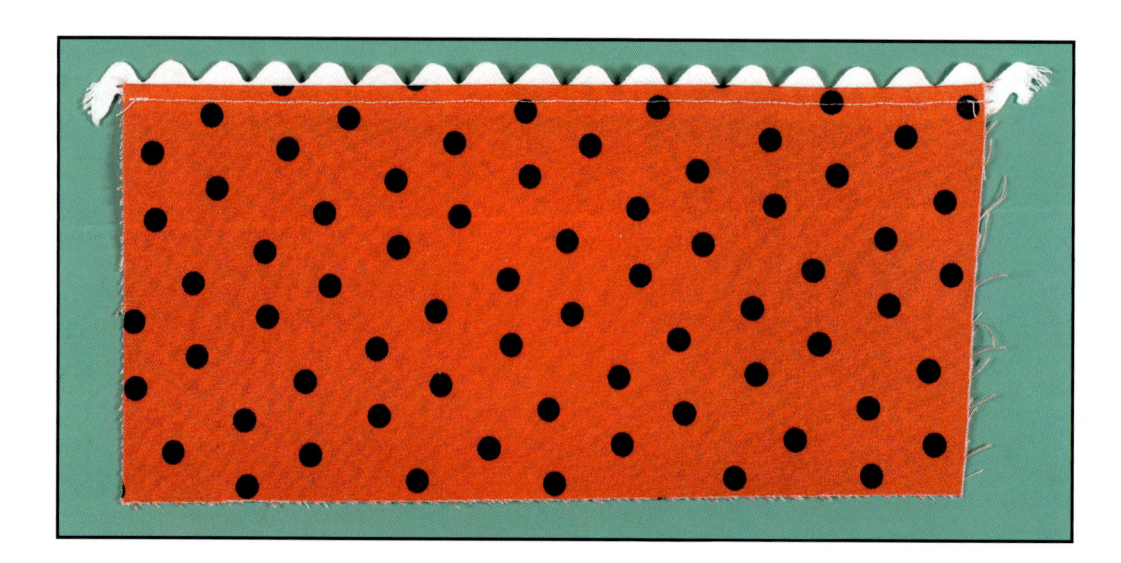

**French Seam**

In a French seam, the raw edges of the fabric are fully enclosed for a neat finish. The seam is first sewn with wrong sides together with a ¼" seam. Then the seam allowances are trimmed and pressed. A second seam is sewn with right sides together with a ½" seam allowance, enclosing the raw edges of the original seam.

**Continuous Bias Strips For Binding**

**Supplies:**
Fabric
Pencil or permanent fabric marking tool
Iron and ironing surface
Clover 1" Bias Tape maker
Sewing machine
Basic sewing supplies

| Length Needed | 2" Wide Bias Strip |
|---|---|
| 110" | 16" x 16" square |
| 220" | 23" x 23" square |
| 340" | 28" x 28" square |
| 480" | 33" x 33" square |

Refer to the chart to find the square fabric size needed to make the desired length of bias binding.

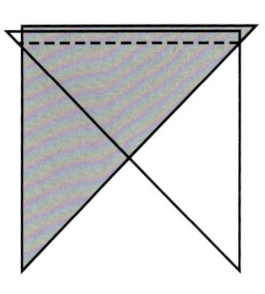

2. With right sides together, sew the triangle with a ¼" seam.

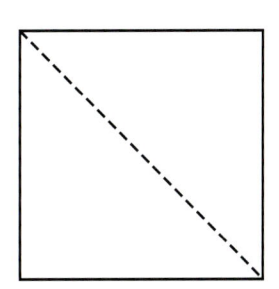

1. Cut the square of fabric in half diagonally.

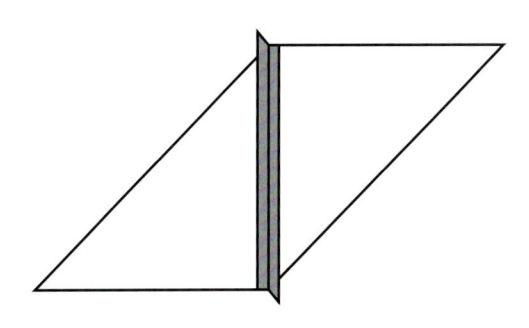

3. Press the seam open.

Teri Henderson Tope  Home Sewn Celebrations

## Tips and Techniques

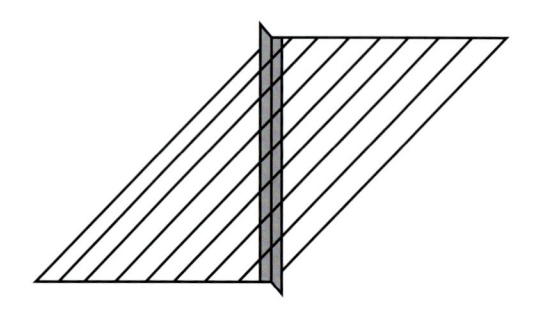

4. On the wrong side of the fabric, draw lines 2" apart to make strips. Use a clear acrylic rotary ruler and a pencil or fine-point permanent pen to draw the lines.

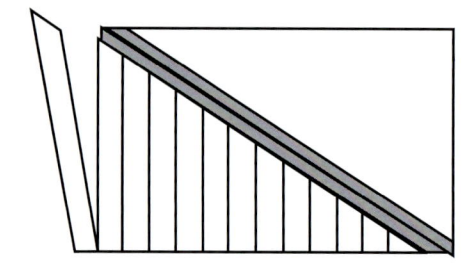

6. Offset the drawn lines by one strip. With right sides together, match lines with pins at the ¼" seam line and stitch. Press this seam open.

With scissors, cut along continuously drawn line.

Following the directions on the 1" Clover Bias Tape Maker, create the bias tape.

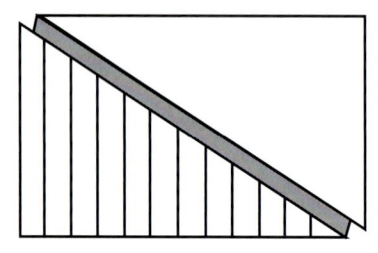

5. Bring the short diagonal edges together, forming a tube.

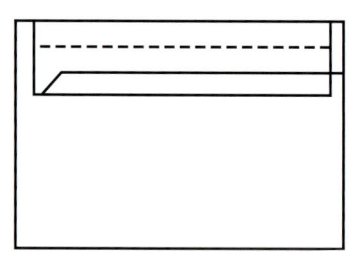

7. Attach bias binding to project with a ¼" seam allowance. Pin bias to the right side of the project and sew along fold.

Teri Henderson Tope — Home Sewn Celebrations

Tips and Techniques

8. Fold remaining bias over project edge and stitch to the back along previously sewn seam.

**Piping**

Make a continuous bias strip following the directions on pages 75–76.

Fold the bias strip in half wrong sides together and lightly press.

Lay cording in the center of the wrong side of the bias strip.

Fold the fabric over the cord, aligning the raw edges.

Using a zipper or piping foot attachment on a sewing machine, sew close to the cord along the length of the strip. The stitching should tightly encase the cord. Trim the seam allowance to ¼" from filled piping.

Cut the length of piping needed for your project plus 4" if joining the ends.

Lay the piping on the right side of the fabric, aligning the raw edges of the piping and the fabric. Position the piping so the corded side faces the center of the project. Pin into place. Using a zipper or piping foot, sew the piping in place.

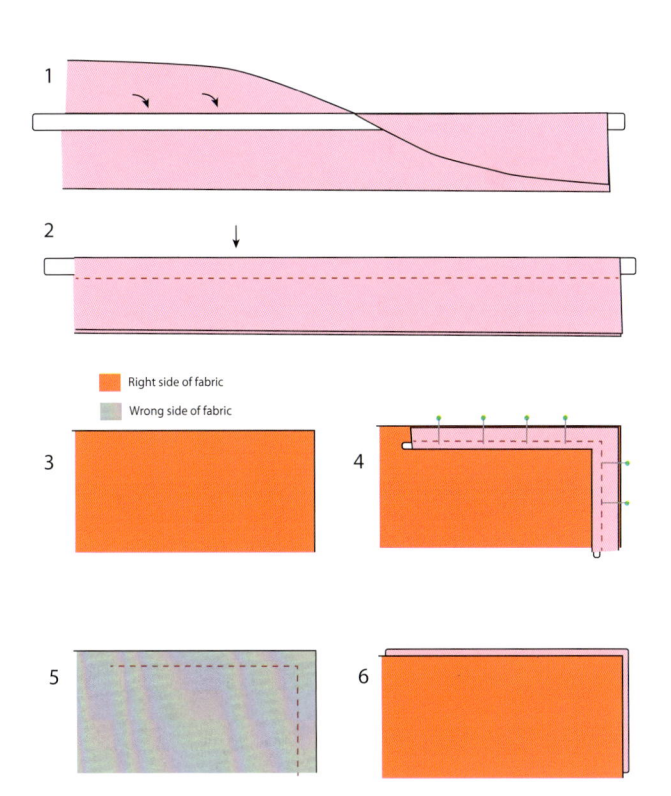

Right side of fabric
Wrong side of fabric

Teri Henderson Tope · Home Sewn Celebrations

Tips and Techniques

**Teri's Basic Sewing Supply List**

These are the items I don't leave town without.
- Fabric scissors—shears, small embroidery, and appliqué scissors
- Paper scissors
- Hand sewing needles
- Straight pins and pincushion
- 1" x 6" acrylic ruler
- 6" x 24" acrylic ruler
- Fabric marking tools and a pencil (Pack several different options so you can mark on anything.)
- Seam ripper
- Extra colors of thread (Toss in white, black, and gray—they go with everything.)
- Masking tape
- Rotary cutter and a mat
- Pressing cloth (In a classroom, you sometimes don't know where that iron has been.)

If you are traveling to a class, double-check to make sure that you have all the cords, feet, extra needles, bobbins, and bobbin case for your sewing machine. Also pack an extra extension cord, just in case!

78     Teri Henderson Tope   Home Sewn Celebrations

# About the Author

## Teri Henderson Tope

Teri Henderson Tope always wanted to be an artist and have a house full of children when she grew up. Well, she became a quilter and her three daughters are nine and five years apart (14 years between the oldest and the youngest) ensuring that there would always be children in her house. You have got to love God's sense of humor.

Always creative, Teri tried every medium available to her from sewing clothes for her Barbie® dolls on an old Singer sewing machine, making macramé plant hangers, 4-H projects, the most unusual Halloween pumpkins and snowmen on the block, to stitching her wedding dress, and then sewing quilts and clothes for her girls.

She found quilting around 1983 and it became her passion and her muse. Her fabric collection grew, as did her frustration with the patterns available to her in the marketplace. Soon she was giving them her Teri Tope Twist and eventually began designing her own original quilts. Bev Young, a local quilt shop owner, encouraged Teri to create patterns based on those designs. Soon Teri was publishing under her company name, maTERIal Girl Designs. To date, she has published over 40 original quilt patterns and has authored a book *Applique in Reverse* published by AQS in 2009.

Teri's infectious love of design, techniques, and fabric has made her a sought-after teacher and lecturer. She has managed to win an award or two for her beautiful quilts, but when asked, she will simply tell you about her love for the process. And if you are lucky, she will pull you into her wonderfully creative and artistic world and maybe even show you a picture of her grandsons.

To view Teri's quilts and patterns, visit her website at www.materialgirldesigns.com.

# More AQS Books

This is only a small selection of the books available from the American Quilter's Society. AQS books are known worldwide for timely topics, clear writing, beautiful color photos, and accurate illustrations and patterns. The following books are available from your local bookseller, quilt shop, or public library.

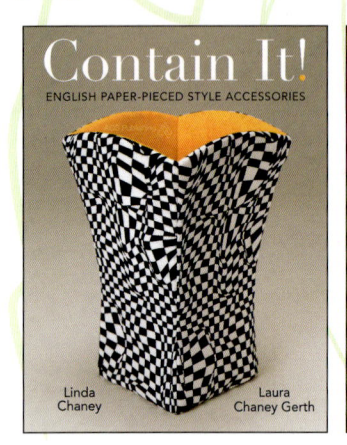

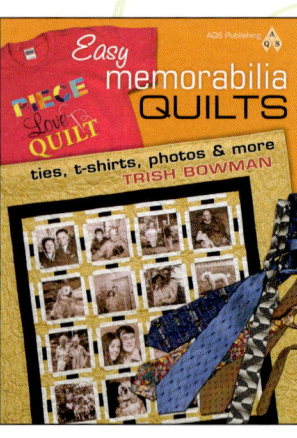

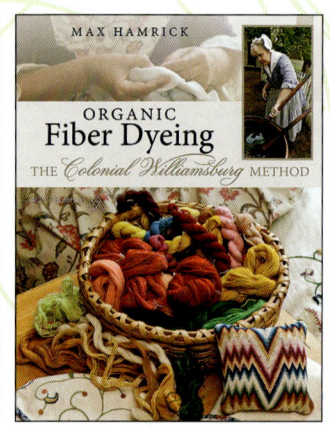

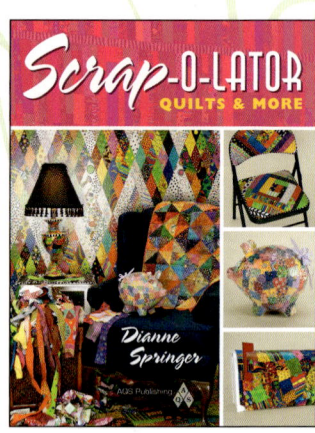

#1543

#1249

#1423

#8665

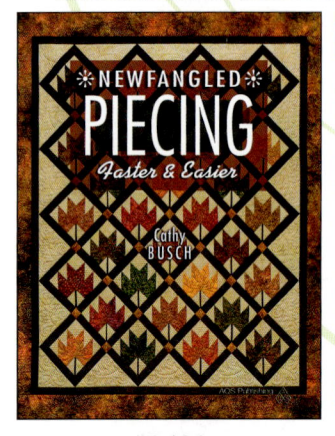

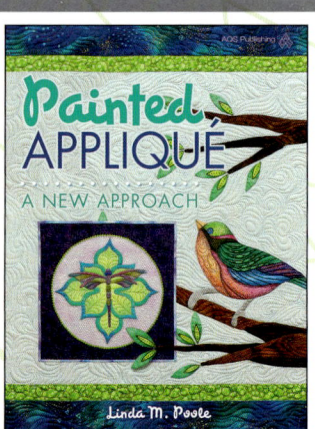

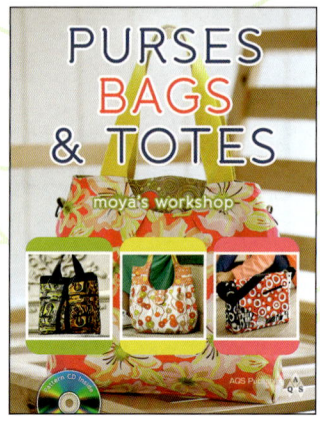

#1420

#1421

#8764

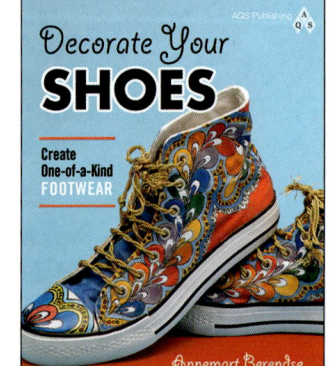

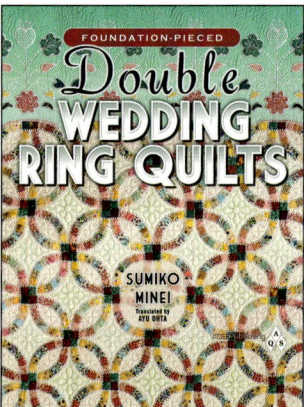

#8766

#8765

**LOOK** for these books nationally.
**CALL** or **VISIT** our website at
www.AmericanQuilter.com
**1-800-626-5420**